Rachel Nicholson

Rachel Nicholson

Alan Wilkinson

Sansom &
Company

This book is dedicated to the memory of
Judith Bumpus and David Hughes

First published in 2010 by Sansom & Company Ltd.,
81G Pembroke Road, Bristol BS8 3EA.
www.sansomandcompany.co.uk

© Alan Wilkinson and Rachel Nicholson

ISBN 978-1-906593-46-9

British Library cataloguing-in-publication data:
A catalogue record for this book is available
from the British Library.

Principal photography of Rachel Nicholson's art by
Bob Berry and John McLean. Photographs of still-life
objects and St Ives motifs © Alan Wilkinson.

Ben Nicholson paintings reproduced on pp.10 and 18
© Angela Verran Taunt 2010. All rights reserved.

Designed by E&P Design, Bath.
Printed and bound by HSW Print Ltd.,
Tonypandy, Rhondda.

Contents

Preface

I MET RACHEL NICHOLSON AT THE Tate Gallery Liverpool in September 1994 at the opening of 'Barbara Hepworth: A Retrospective', which I co-curated, but it was not until 2005, when I began semi-annual visits to St Ives, that we became friends. I usually stay at 18 Barnaloft, overlooking Porthmeor Beach, in the same building where Rachel has a flat. One evening she told me her recollections of Piet Mondrian coming for tea in Hampstead (it was some time between September 1938 and the end of August 1939) with her parents Ben Nicholson and Barbara Hepworth, and thinking how very rude of him, as he licked his knife. It was such a vivid and unexpected image of the Dutchman, who has been described as looking more like scientist or priest than an artist, that I thought we should do a taped interview to record other memories, particularly of her parents, of St Ives and her career as an artist. This book could have been dedicated 'To Mondrian's knife'. It was the contents of the interview (p.27), which was recorded in St Ives on 27 April 2008, that suggested to me that a serious study of Rachel's art was overdue. Previous publications consist of modest catalogues of three London exhibitions at Montpelier Studio, 1994, and Montpelier Sandelson, 1997 and 2000, and the more substantial catalogue of Rachel's one-man show at Caroline Wiseman Modern Art, in 2006.

In addition to the interview, the other major texts are the introduction, the earlier published assessments, and the appreciations by friends, family, curators, collectors and dealers. In writing to ask friends *et al* to consider contributing their thoughts, I suggested anything from a few sentences to 270 words, the length of Lincoln's Gettysburg Address. I am most grateful to the contributors; their short essays greatly enhance our appreciation of the captivating magic of Rachel's art.

I would like to thank friends and colleagues for their help and suggestions: Madeleine Bessborough, Sophie Bowness, Agnes Davis, Dell Casdagli, Fenella Clemens, Mary and Malcolm Cochrane, Patzi Craven, Emma Earl, Frederica Freer, Joanna Lagneau, Jeremy Lewison, Fiona Sampson, Chris Stephens, Michael Tooby, Margaret Walker and Caroline Wiseman. I am grateful to John Sansom for his interest and support in publishing this book, another of his major monographs on important artists working in Cornwall.

Rachel Nicholson has devoted so much time to this project during the past year that her painting has suffered, but I hope that the book will have been worth the effort and endless distractions. We selected together the paintings and prints illustrated here, as well as the family photographs. I am most grateful to Rachel for her hospitality, for her tireless dedication and her patience in answering my many questions about her life and art. Her husband, Dr Michael Kidd, and their grand-daughter Felix Kidd, have been extremely helpful in sorting out the digital, computer images of the paintings, a task far beyond the very limited technological skills of the artist and author.

Alan Wilkinson

Rachel in her London studio, 2006

PHOTOGRAPH BY BRIAN USHER

Still Life on Navy Blue
(1979)
oil, 30.5 x 38.1 cm

Introduction

'Each perturbation smooth'd
with outward calm'
JOHN MILTON, *PARADISE LOST*

IN JUNE OF 1980, RACHEL'S FATHER, Ben Nicholson, turned up unannounced at Montpelier Studio to view his daughter's first London exhibition and remarked to gallery owner Bernice Sandelson of *Still Life on Navy Blue*, 1979 (left): 'I had never realised she could paint so well. I would have been happy to have painted that one myself.' No subsequent praise of her work by friend or family, artist or curator, collector or critic could have possibly meant as much to Rachel Nicholson as her father's spontaneous reaction to one of her early still-life pictures, executed just four years after she had embarked on a career as an artist. With the daunting heritage on her father's side of two generations of Nicholson artists, and on her mother's, of a famous sculptor, it is remarkable how quickly and with such assurance, Rachel had absorbed the still-life motif of Ben, and created a distinctive and unmistakable style of her own. As Harold Bloom remarked in *The Anxiety of Influence* (1973), 'Weaker talents idealize; figures of capable imagination appropriate for themselves.'

Rachel, one of eight of the third generation of Britain's most prominent family of artists, summed up her thirty-year career in *A Vital Simplicity: Four Generations of the Nicholson Family* (Caroline Wiseman, 2004):

I am a self-taught artist who started painting in my early forties when my youngest child was seven years old (I have three children). My paintings are a way of trying to bring about a sense of peace, and the hope that this will extend to the viewer. The arrangement of objects, and how they look outside my paintings, i.e. in the house, and then extending to my paintings is central to my work. I have, of course, inherited the love of still-life objects from my father, and he from William. Also important to my work is a love of landscape and seascapes and into these I often incorporate jugs, cups and spoons etc. I hope the thread of the still-life theme can be seen through this current exhibition.

Although Rachel began her career in 1975, the year that her mother, Barbara Hepworth, died, the two events were, the artist maintains, unrelated. It was in that year she moved with her family to Leicestershire and as she commented in our interview: 'My youngest child was at primary school and I just had a little bit of time, a little window of opportunity.' But there was, however, a tangible link with her mother's pictorial work, although this was not, as some have surmised, the catalyst that launched her career. 'When Barbara died,' Rachel told me, 'she left a few oil paints, which were passed on to me.' And likewise, when Ben Nicholson died in 1982, she was given some of the oil paints from his Hampstead studio, as well as, in his will, two still-life objects, which joined the dozen or so items that her father had given to her over the years. (A number of these are illustrated

Ben Nicholson
1943–5 (St Ives, Cornwall)
oil and pencil on canvas board,
40.6 x 50.2 cm
TATE

in this book.) Apart from her collection of paintings, drawings and sculptures by Ben and Barbara, as Rachel called her parents, it would be difficult to imagine more palpable ties with her Nicholson/Hepworth legacy.

Still-life objects were the subject of Rachel's first paintings and looking back on the work of thirty-five years, I would say that still lifes, not landscapes, have been 'the more fundamental obsession,' to borrow Henry Moore's phrase with which he defined the slight edge in his work that the mother and child motif had over the reclining figure. Indeed, as Rachel told me recently, 'The still life was more inbuilt, inherited, what I started with.' In recent years, more and more of her landscapes and views of townscapes, seascapes or landscapes through windows and doors, include in the foreground an array of bowls, jugs, mugs, glasses, spoons and forks, teacups and saucers, tea pots and decanters. Anyone who has visited Rachel in her London studio can not help but notice on shelves and other surfaces, the orderly arrangement of her extensive collection and their relationship to each other, as well as their separateness. Rachel reckons there are several hundred items in her collection. With very few exceptions (the early *Still Life*

with Red Stripe on Grey, 1977 (p.65), is one of them) in her still-life pictures the objects very rarely touch, unlike the overlapping mugs, cups and jugs in some of Ben Nicholson's early pictures of the 1920s, and in his Cornish still life/landscape paintings of the 1940s, such as *1943–5 (St Ives, Cornwall)*. 'I think I am always going to be interested in the relationship of objects,' Rachel commented in 1994. 'People say I am too tidy, but what they don't understand is that I see everything placed in relationship to something else – at home or on the canvas.'

IN *JUG AND CUP ON GREEN*, 1975, ONE of the earliest still lifes, the jug and small cup sit side by side parallel to the picture plane, and are more or less centred on the green, rectangular background, which projects forward from the horizontal band of white, and the two much narrower stripes at the top and at the bottom of the picture. The two objects are shown in profile, as it were, so that spaces are fully visible between the handles and the jug and the cup. This small gouache not only announces the birth of the still-life motif at the outset of Rachel's career, it also establishes one of her favourite

Jug and Cup on Green
(1975)
gouache, 26.1 x 33 cm

Glass with Spoon on Blue
(1978)
oil, 33 x 17.8 cm

compositional arrangements; that of placing the still-life objects on a central, horizontal background. A very similar positioning of the six separate bands of background colours is repeated thirty years later in *Green Tea Pot with Julia's Jug*, 2005/6 (p.127). *Glass with Spoon on Blue*, 1978, the first picture that Rachel sold, was bought by Mary Pearce, the mother of Bryan, 'the miracle painter of St Ives.' The way in which the glass is positioned directly above the spoon is typical of a number of the early still-life compositions. In the still-life pictures, and in the later landscapes, which began in earnest in 1984/5, drawing the objects or the *plein air* motif was and has remained the first stage in the creative process. Both still lifes and landscapes are painted in the studio. With the still lifes, I asked Rachel if, after the drawing was completed, she painted the objects first or the background: 'In the old days, I would start to paint the background and then the objects; now I paint the still-life objects first.'

The still life theme has not only been 'the more fundamental obsession', it is also the genre which has strong associations with the work of her grandfather, William Nicholson, and her father, Ben. The ties are not, however, simply thematic, but are linked to the family history of the objects themselves. The glasses, tea cups, mugs, jugs, a glass decanter and other items that Rachel had been given or inherited from Ben, are, as

Barbara Hepworth's coffee pot and Japanese fork and spoons

Ben Nicholson's Man Friday mug, flowered mug and mug with letters

Rachel's collection of Ben Nicholson's still life objects

Ben's Mug with Letters
(1999/2008)
oil, 29.6 x 24.2 cm

Michael Tooby pointed out, 'loaded with memory and association… It is as if she is remaking for herself her father's depiction of her grandfather's collection of objects for still lifes.' Or, as Chris Stephens remarked, '*A Nicholson Jug* [1992; for the 2004 version of the same jug, see p.oo] acknowledged what many people might be thinking on seeing yet another painter called Nicholson painting that same vessel.' Most of the objects that her parents once owned and which now belong to Rachel, came from her father. In some of her still lifes, the previous owner is identified in the title, as above, and in *Ben's Mug with Letters*, 1999/2008. In other pictures, such as *Theme on Striped Tea Cup and Flowered Mug*, 1992 (p.96), it was the artist who told me that the mug (p.13) belonged to Ben. The coffee pot (p.12) belonged to Barbara,

as did the wooden Japanese spoons and forks of varying lengths that appear frequently in Rachel's work (p.12). Barbara had acquired them from Janet Leach. Rachel thinks that the brown jug in *Restaurant View with Leach Jug*, 1998 (p.117), probably belonged to her mother. Her parents are symbolically reunited in *Barbara's Coffee Pot and Ben's Mug*, 2005/08 (p.100).

Rachel mentioned that her still life pictures take longer to do, which suggests to me that they represent a more concentrated and intense effort than the landscapes, and indeed I find that they are bolder and stronger. In the landscapes, seascapes and townscapes, the fields and hills, the sea, beach and rocks, and the buildings of St Ives are fixed entities that to a large extent dictate the layout of the composition. In the still lifes, on the other

Still Life with Pink Square
(1985)
gouache, 22.2 x 29.3 cm

hand, the artist has complete freedom in the shapes, textures and colours of the abstract backgrounds, in the selection of object or objects, and in their positioning on the picture plane, from a single item, as in *Jug with Blue Stripe*, 2004, to *Sextet*, 2006. There are countless compositional choices and decisions to be made. In the still lifes, Rachel's imagination is at its most free and inventive, open to flights of fancy and pictorial invention. Jugs, cups, spoons and tea pots are crisply delineated with a precision and an eye for the detailed surface patterns that is not required in the generally flat, unmodulated areas of colour in the landscapes and townscapes. In selecting with Rachel the pictures for this book, I was astonished at the richness and variety of the abstract, still-life backgrounds, from a favourite format

Habitat bowl

Orkneys No.2
(1982)
gouache, 21.8 x 29.3 cm

from the beginning, that of *Jug and Cup on Green*, 1975, the Ben Nicholsonesque series of rectangles in *Still Life with Pink Square*, 1985 (p.15), the mottled texture of the central band in *Still life on Smoky Blue*, 1984 (p.81), the scratched (with her finger, not with a razor blade as Ben had used) surface of *Goblet with Curtains*, 1983 (p.74), to the irregular, angular forms in *Brown and Grey Coffee Jug*, 1981 (p.72), which are distinctly reminiscent of the asymmetrical shapes of Ben's reliefs and prints. The titles of the still lifes vary. Some, such as *Jug and Cup on Yellow*, 1978 (p.66), identify the objects and describe the background colour. In others, such as *Green and Brown*, 2003/05, the title refers only to the colours of the two still-life objects. *Ben's Mug with Letters*, 1999/2008 (p.14), identifies the previous owner and describes the object.

Human figures are absent from Rachel's art, and perhaps the mugs, jugs and cups are, on a subconscious level, surrogate presences for them. Her son, Jeremy Kidd, noted that just as portraits often resemble the artist who painted them, his mother's still-life objects 'are reflections or projections of something in her character and perhaps desire for family.' Of the positioning of the still life objects, Chris Stephens commented that 'their arrangement has a slight awkwardness, as if each is embarrassed in the company of the others.' Andrea Frears sees in the wavy bands of colour, 'an abstracted form of tide on shore, upon which her composition of cups and milk jugs lurch slightly.' For Katherine Smalley, 'In the still-life paintings, the objects feel like characters in a play, finely choreographed in truth and tension...'

Mug and Spoon in Landscape
(1978)
oil, 24.2 x 38.8 cm

MUG AND SPOON IN LANDSCAPE, 1978 – Rachel's earliest landscape – was, she thinks, an imaginary one. A view through a window onto a landscape, seascape or townscape was a favourite motif in Ben Nicholson's early St Ives pictures, such as *1930 (Porthmeor window – looking out to sea)*, and in his Cornish still life/landscape paintings of the 1940s, as in *1943–5 (St Ives, Cornwall)* (p.10). *Mug and Spoon in Landscape* not only marks the first break with the still-life pictures of the previous three years, it heralds in a rudimentary form what was to become in the mid-1980s and has remained a dominant theme in Rachel's work; the inside/outside views of landscapes, seascapes and townscapes, from various interior, usually domestic, settings.

Orkneys No.1, 1982, the first observed landscape, was followed by *Orkneys No.2* (left). Over the years, Rachel has produced landscape paintings of these islands off the north-east coast of Scotland, to ones of the Isles of Scilly, some thirty miles south-west of Land's End. In between – in both time and place – she has made groups of works depicting Cumbria, Yorkshire, Derbyshire, Nottinghamshire, Sussex, Dorset and west Cornwall landscapes. The two Orkney pictures were isolated examples; her first concentrated landscape efforts date from 1984, of which *Derbyshire No.1*, 1984 (p.35), is the earliest. It seems to me that the fields, with their flat, unmodulated areas of colour and pronounced outlines, owe an obvious debt to Nicholson's *faux naïve* landscapes of the 1920s, but even more so to later paintings, such as *1940 (Cornish landscape)* (p.18). Both Ben's and Rachel's pictures represent, no doubt fortuitously, a form of latter-day

Ben Nicholson
1940 (Cornish landscape)
oil, tempera and pencil on board,
25.4 x 35.6 cm

View from Trencrom
(1986)
gouache, 36.8 x 47 cm

Cloisonism, that style of French painting of the late 1880s, exemplified in the work of Anquetin, Toulouse-Lautrec, van Gogh and Bernard, in which flattened areas of colour surrounded by strong contour lines replaced traditional perspective and modelling. In the earliest pure landscapes, those of Derbyshire and Nottinghamshire (p.78), executed between 1984 and 1986, and in the first Cornish landscapes of 1985–86, such as *View from Trencrom*, 1986, the colours, especially the greens and browns, are much darker and more sombre than in the later works. Rachel mixes her colours and, for example, in painting the sea, she may combine three or four shades of blue with several greys, white and olive green. For a self-taught artist, the delicately balanced tonality of the landscapes is a remarkable achievement.

Rachel began by depicting still-life objects in interior spaces, with a view through a window onto the landscape beyond, as early as *Mug and Spoon in Landscape*, 1978, mentioned above. But since the mid-1980s, these fragile, domestic items inhabit the landscape itself, of which *Blue Jug with Landscape*, 1984, is probably the earliest. One of my favourite outdoor still lifes is *Near Eagles Nest*, 1996 (right). In the foreground, beside a lonely stretch of road between St Ives and Zennor, Rachel has created a patterned diagonal table or shelf

for the knife, tea cup and glass, perhaps hoping that Patrick Heron might stop by for tea. There is a curious sense of displacement, what Judith Bumpus calls 'the slightly surreal surprise,' which gives the viewer a mild visual jolt, in that the delicate still-life objects have been removed from their familiar context, but nothing as outrageous or unexpected as the poet Isidore Ducasse's famous image that had such obvious appeal to the Surrealists: 'as beautiful as the chance meeting on a dissecting table of a sewing machine and an umbrella.'

If the still lifes are the most powerful and direct of Rachel's work, whose objects have been painted with such loving and precise care, the inside/outside paintings that began in earnest in mid-1985 are, with their complex architectural geometry, spatially her most demanding pictures. Apart from several works from the late 1970s and early 1980s, such as *Mug and Spoon with Landscape*, 1978, the motif was a new one. What I refer to as the inside/outside pictures do not simply depict a view through a narrow window frame bordering the frame of the picture itself, as in *Winter Landscape with Jug and Glass*, 1981 (p.20), but present an interior setting of greater compositional weight than the view looking out through windows and doors. The new challenge was to master the geometry of the architectural spaces.

Near Eagles Nest
(1996)
gouache, 22.9 x 29.7 cm

Winter Landscape with Jug and Glass
(1981)
oil, 33.7 x 40.6 cm

Inevitably, perhaps, still-life objects inhabit the domestic interiors. In St Ives, Rachel has painted inside/outside views from her Barnaloft flat onto Porthmeor beach, but more often from the small studio flat that belonged to Barbara Hepworth, on the top level of the building. She also asked several friends in the town if she could do some preparatory drawings of views from inside their flats and houses. *View from the Saltings*, 1994 (right), affords the prospect from the eastern end of Porthmeor Beach, of the sand at centre left, and of the headland and Clodgy Point. In *Slantways* 2, 2004 (p.22), which looks out on the relatively protected harbour, the view framed by the window could almost be read, as Fenella Clemens, the owner of the picture, has pointed out (p.49), as a very large Rachel Nicholson hanging on the wall. In writing of one of Rachel's views from the elevated Tate St Ives restaurant (pp.23, 110, 111 and 117) Chris Stephens perceptively observed: 'For those interested in ideas of art and place, there can be few subjects more stimulating than a Nicholson jug set against the Tate's panoramic view of the artists' colony of St Ives over which her parents so famously presided.'

View from the Saltings
(1994)
acrylic, 30.5 x 40.6 cm

CLARE AND ERIC ASH

View from the Saltings

View from Tate St Ives restaurant

In the almost two hundred years since J.M.W. Turner visited St Ives in 1811 and made four drawings in a sketch book, the town, its harbour, Porthmeor Beach and the Atlantic Ocean, have been the subjects of works by an astonishing number of artists, of whom the most celebrated are James McNeil Whistler, Walter Sickert, Alfred Wallis, Christopher Wood, Ben Nicholson, Victor Pasmore, Wilhelmina Barns-Graham, Patrick Heron, and Terry Frost. But for me, the two painters who have appropriated the town in the way in which Canaletto owns Venice, and Utrillo the streets of Paris, are Bryan Pearce (1929–2007) and Rachel Nicholson. Apart from the still-life pictures, St Ives motifs, and to a lesser extent the landscape of the Penwith peninsula of west Cornwall, have been the epicentre of her art since the mid-1980s.

Slantways 2
(2004)
gouache, 29.9 x 40.6 cm
FENELLA CLEMENS

Tate View from Corner Window 2
(1998)
acrylic, 50.8 x 61 cm

View of St Ives from the Garrack Hotel

As one of the third generation of Nicholson artists, Rachel has not only extended and enriched the family tradition, she has altered our perception of it. I now see Ben's *1940 (Cornish landscape)* not only as an early example of his return to landscape painting soon after he arrived in Carbis Bay, but as representative of the work that inspired Rachel's first efforts in this genre. One does not simply associate the subject of *A Nicholson Jug*, 1992, with Ben, its previous owner. Rachel's depiction of the jug (p.25) in several pictures has extended its history and significance. For me, part of the fascination of Rachel's work is, on the one hand, the continuity and enrichment of her Nicholson heritage and, on the other, the captivating accessibility and charm of her pictures, to which the contributions written for this book give ample affirmation. Several years ago, an American collector, who had never heard of the artist, came to my flat for a drink, saw *The Island with Decanter* 2005/07 (p.139) and bought one of her pictures in London a few days later. With Rachel's work, it is often love at first sight.

AT THE END OF OUR INTERVIEW, I asked Rachel if she thought that my phrase 'the geometry of peace and tranquillity' was an apposite description of her work. She agreed that it was, and added that Barbara Hepworth's 'sculptures often give me this feeling of peace, so maybe we were both looking for the same thing.'

In reading through the appreciations of Rachel's art in this book, I was struck by how certain descriptive words are repeated and sprinkled throughout. *Peace* and *tranquillity* are used again, but not together. *Quiet* appears three times and *quietness* once, each in different essays. Concepts of balance, of calm, and of freshness of vision are each used twice, again each time by different authors. It seems appropriate that *simplicity*, which Richard Morphet included in his title for the exhibition catalogue *A Vital Simplicity: Four Generations of the Nicholson Family*, 2004, may be found in three of the essays.

To borrow from Walter Savage Landor's poem 'Finis', 'Nature I loved and, next to Nature, Art', English literature I loved and, next to English, art history. I have chosen some lines of prose and poetry that came to mind as I was working on this book. As with the words of the contributors singled out above, I hope that they will enhance or at least complement the reader's appreciation of Rachel Nicholson's unique and serene vision:

Thomas Hardy's 'the landscape bore that impress of reserve, taciturnity,' reflects the quiet calm and restraint of Rachel's pictures.

John Betjeman's 'Stones in every fertile place / Little fields with boulders dotted' reminded me immediately of the landscapes of the Penwith peninsula, such as *Near Eagles Nest* 1996 (p.19).

Ben Nicholson's Mocha ware jug

Jug with Blue Stripe
(2004)
oil, 30.5 x 25.4 cm

William Wordsworth's 'The innocent brightness of a new-born Day / Is lovely yet' could very well describe the freshness and deceptive simplicity of the landscapes.

Lord Byron's 'Of cloudless climes…' echoes the clear and cloudless skies that are a feature of almost all of Rachel's *plein air* pictures.

Matthew Arnold's 'The sea is calm to-night' is exactly how the Atlantic Ocean or St Ives Bay appears in the seascapes.

Anne Wilkinson's:

No wind at all
On the wide green world
Where fields go stroll-
ing by

Porthmeor Beach

mirrors the almost eerie stillness and quietness of Rachel's imaginary world.

I shall end by focusing on Rachel herself and to a word that was used quite independently in two of the appreciations. Her friends, Clare and Eric Ash, commented: 'Above all the seeing eye has a *twinkle* [my italics]. The observer is quite human.' St Ives artist Naomi Frears perceptively observed a quite enchanting aspect of the artist's character, something I had noticed but had never articulated: 'Rachel might seem to be a little shy and serious if you didn't know her, but is in fact a person with a naughty twinkle in her eye.' Although Rachel was reminded that Ben produced from time to time such disarming expressions, to her friends at least, she is the Nicholson who has perfected the art of the mischievous twinkle.

Interview

Alan Wilkinson: We are in 18 Barnaloft overlooking Porthmeor Beach, in the flat that your mother, Barbara Hepworth, bought in 1962 as a studio for drawing and as accommodation for friends and family. Let's begin at the beginning. In the autumn of 1934 your parents Ben Nicholson and Barbara Hepworth, who were living in Hampstead, were expecting a baby. On 3 October triplets arrived. In what order were you, Simon and Sarah born?

Rachel Nicholson: My brother Simon was born the first, I was second and my sister Sarah the third. However, I was the smallest.

And you weighed?

Two and three-quarter pounds.

Growing up as a triplet, was it a very different feeling to just having a brother or sister of a different age?

Well, I suppose we probably didn't know what it was like not to be three, but I think that three is quite a difficult number. You tend to, you know, either be getting on with one or the other, but three together doesn't work all that well.

What are your earliest memories of Hampstead, where you lived from 1934 until late August 1939 when you and your family moved to Carbis Bay on the outskirts of St Ives? Do you have many memories of London; you were only five I suppose when you left.

Well, not quite five – we would have been five on 3 October. So, I don't remember an enormous amount. I have memories of being taken by our nurse to Primrose Hill, all three of us, for daily walks and I recall a few little things about the studio. The three of us slept up in a little balcony room and, of course, it was an open studio down below, and there was a small garden with a little hut.

Did your parents share a studio or did they each have their own working space?

Well, they were in a separate studio, a few doors down and we had a nurse and a cook living in our studio. I do remember the barrage balloons that you could see out of the window, which I was a little bit frightened of, so my father called them 'George and Harry', probably in order to try to make them a little less frightening! Later I think he had a work space on the other side of the path running past the Mall Studios.

You told me a wonderful story about Piet Mondrian coming for tea.

Yes, the two people I do remember visiting the studio would have been Mondrian and John Skeaping, my mother's first husband, and Mondrian did come to tea. I don't recall a lot about Mondrian, but I do remember him putting a knife in his mouth and being rather shocked, because we had been brought up to understand that that was very bad manners. I wish I could remember more about him.

Didn't Ben and Barbara try to entice Mondrian to come to Cornwall?

Yes, I think they did. They persuaded Naum and Miriam Gabo, but I think Mondrian was

Sarah, Rachel and Simon Hepworth-Nicholson, 1935

Simon, Rachel and Sarah,
Carbis Bay beach, 1940s

really a town person and he couldn't be persuaded, which was rather a shame. He went to New York instead.

Henry and Irina Moore were neighbours. They lived at 11a Parkhill Road. Do you remember them?
No I don't. The person whom I do remember is John Cecil Stephenson who lived next door at 6 The Mall Studios. He had a recent retrospective at the Fine Art Society, London. He used to make model trains. They were quite big, and he would allow us to sit on one of these trains and go up and down the Mall on it, which we thoroughly enjoyed. Other than that, I just have faint memories of the day we left for Cornwall. I seem to recall there was a pillar in the studio, in the room, and I think we remembered after we had set off that my father had left one of those old-fashioned watches, pocket watches, with a chain hanging, I think, on a nail on the pillar. We had to say goodbye to that one. The only other memory I have about the trip was my father getting tired and we stopped somewhere on the journey and he went off, disappeared and had a little rest and came back refreshed. We were a little bit worried as to whether he was going to reappear, but anyway...

As a young girl were you interested in painting and sculpture? Were there art lessons at school that you particularly enjoyed?
Well, I did art at school. Unfortunately it was just after the war so materials were very scarce and all we had was powder paint and I actually loathed powder paint. I really wanted something thicker which I never had. So, I suppose I didn't enjoy it a great deal, but then I didn't really have any confidence in my own abilities.

Did your parents encourage you at all to follow in their footsteps?
I would say not really. (Laughs)

But your brother Simon became a sculptor. Did Ben and Barbara encourage him?
He didn't really become a sculptor. Well, I suppose his objects were three-dimensional in the sense that he made these objects with anything that came to hand, like ice-cream sticks or felt pads and other everyday things. I would call them objects. And he was good at drawing. He spent one year at the Royal College of Art because he was rejected for National Service as he was asthmatic and therefore had a year to spare before he went up to Cambridge. Later he became very

Ben Nicholson

Rachel aged about three

Barbara Hepworth

interested in art and the environment, and in art education, especially for children.

Were your parents quite happy for him to become an artist?
Simon studied archaeology and anthropology at Cambridge, after spending one year at the Royal College of Art. My mother would, perhaps, have liked him to have completed his PhD. I imagine they were both happy for him to be involved in art in some way.

What about music? I think you told me that Sarah and Simon studied music but you didn't.
Simon didn't, in fact, but my mother hoped he would play the violin. Perhaps there was a violin on loan or something like that. Sarah and I were not actually encouraged to play but my sister had a different tutor to me at school and he went down to see my mother when Sarah was fourteen or fifteen, to persuade my mother to allow her to play the flute, which she subsequently studied.

And she still plays, doesn't she?
Yes. She went to the Arts Department, Dartington Hall and then on to London and the Guildhall School of Music.

But music was a great love of your mother's was it not?
It was.

And your father's as well, or not so much?
I think he liked music. I don't think it was so important to him.

You and your family, a cook and a nanny arrived in Carbis Bay, 25 August 1939. It was Adrian Stokes and his wife Margaret Mellis who suggested you come down and stay with them, wasn't it?
Well, they were very kind because they put us up at their house, Little Parc Owles.

Yes, until you moved on 27 December. Do you remember Little Parc Owles?
I don't remember much. I think perhaps I recall running around outside. Otherwise I don't really remember it. I think Barbara had the use of a garage space at the bottom of the garden.

And then you moved to a house nearby.
We then rented a rather decrepit house.

Dunluce?
Yes. Then in September, 1942, when we were almost eight, we moved to Chy-an-Kerris in

Simon Nicholson

Headland Road in Carbis Bay, which overlooked the whole of St Ives Bay.

You had more or less the same view that Virginia Woolf loved as a child.
I suppose her view would have been a little bit different because Talland House, which her father Leslie Stephen rented, was actually in St Ives above the railway station. In summer, the view of the bay was absolutely wonderful.

And across St Ives Bay you could see Godrevy lighthouse, which inspired Virginia Woolf's novel *To the Lighthouse*.
Oh, yes. You could see the whole bay.

Did your parents each have their own studio when they moved?
When we moved to Chy-an-Kerris my father had a room on the second floor, facing the sea for his work, and my mother had the one underneath, facing the sea, which was on the ground floor and she did her sculpture out in the back yard.

Your mother wrote that the view from her studio was, 'towards the horizon of the sea and enfolded (but with always the escape for the eye straight out to the Atlantic) by the arms of land to the left and right of me.' This view inspired *Pelagos*, 1946, wood with painted interior and strings, which is for me one of her most beautiful carvings.

I would agree. Well, I am not surprised because the view was so stunning in the summer.

You told me that you weren't allowed into your parents' studios.
Well, occasionally my father would let me just walk in and briefly watch him at work. My mother definitely not! I think that was her territory and she definitely didn't want us in it, which I now find much more understandable!

Memories of artist friends of your parents in St Ives. I don't suppose you ever ran into Alfred Wallis, who died in 1942.
No.

But were you aware, as a young girl, of Wallis's paintings? Ben and Barbara owned quite a number, which they bought directly from the old, retired fisherman.
No, I wasn't. Maybe they didn't have them framed.

Perhaps they just left them on the bits of card they were painted on. You must remember Naum and Miriam Gabo. They had arrived in Carbis Bay by 15 September 1939 about three weeks after you did and moved into Faerystones, a short walk from Little Parc Owles.
Yes, I do.

Rachel at Dartington Hall School

And their daughter Nina-Serafima, who was born on 26 May 1941.
Yes, there was a great deal of excitement when Nina arrived. I remember going over to see her soon after she was born. One of the things I do remember, when we were living at Dunluce, was Gabo going up to London to give a broadcast and we looked after Snezhka, his dog, which we thought was wonderful.

Snezhka, translation from the Russian, snowball?
I think it is 'snowball' – I could be wrong.

Are there any other artists whom you particularly remember, Peter Lanyon or Patrick Heron, perhaps?
Well, my father took me to tea once or twice to see Peter Lanyon and quite a lot later they were friendly with John Forrester, whom I think was a New Zealand painter, who was in St Ives for a while. And then, of course, there was John Wells, who would sometimes spend Christmas with us.

Yes, Wells worked for your mother for several years. What of Bernard Leach?
Not a lot of Bernard Leach at that time, but certainly later. But, we did visit his son, David Leach and we played table tennis with him and his sons.

Did you just go to a local school? In 1939 you were hardly old enough for school.

Well, I didn't go to school until I was eight, as we were taught by our nurse, and then we went to this small school called Brush End, which had been evacuated from the New Forest to Carbis Bay. I went for a couple of years and then at ten we went to Dartington.

In 1949 your mother bought Trewyn Studio in the centre of St Ives, which is now the Barbara Hepworth Museum. As there wasn't room for the three of you there, you lived across the road.
Yes, she bought a little cottage so when we came for a holiday, we were self-supporting.

Were your parents affectionate? You said Ben could be difficult at times? I met your mother once. She was quite shy. We talked mainly about her drawings.
Oh, really. Well my father, of course, had a good sense of humour, always cracking jokes, puns and so on. It was nice for us because if he got to a break in his work, he would come and play ball games. Occasionally he would come down into what was, I suppose, the sitting room, although it was hardly ever used as such, and played some games. The family didn't really do anything communal. Otherwise it was used when there were visitors. My mother on the whole really only, as far as I can remember, emerged for meals, and a day or two at Christmas.

Dr Michael Kidd and Rachel's engagement party, 1960

You said that Barbara used to work non-stop.
Yes, but my father's way of working was very different. I mean he would go off to have a game of golf on the Lelant golf course, because in a way he was thinking about work and it would give him ideas. They both worked enormously hard.

What were the other games that Ben enjoyed? You mentioned diabolo and ping pong. I'm not familiar with the former.
Diabolo is a game played with a two-headed top, which is spun, tossed and caught on a string attached to two sticks. My father always said his chief claim to fame was winning a competition at the Crystal Palace when he was, I believe, fifteen! I think it was an international competition. He also invented his own game of ping pong and, you know, we didn't have an actual ping pong table, so he invented this game, which would work on the table he'd made, partly as an air-raid shelter for the family to get under if there should be an air raid.

Ben loved tennis. Did you play as well?
They hadn't invented these wonderful sponge rubber tennis balls which, when I think about it, we could have played on the beach, and we didn't have enough money to rent a court. I only remember doing so once, at a tennis court down the road. Ben impressed on me that it was very important to play all the right strokes and so on. However, I believe he played with Andras Kalman and went to Wimbledon with Andras to watch the tennis.

You mentioned that you liked cricket.
Yes, I played cricket at school at Dartington and also football. Sarah also played cricket. I was good at bowling and Sarah at batting.

Oh good! Virginia Woolf, as I told you, loved cricket. There is a photograph of her, aged five, playing cricket with her siblings. You also mentioned that you played with gramophone records on the beach.
Well I think Ben would sometimes go down onto Lelant beach, and occasionally we went, too, and would throw a gramophone record, which was the nearest thing to a frisbee in those days. What a shame that the plastic frisbees hadn't been invented at that time because we would have had great fun. We sometimes played ball games with Ben in the road, which wasn't appreciated by the neighours!

Your mother loathed ball games but loved dancing?
Yes.

Alison and Jeremy Kidd, late 1960s

Julia Kidd, mid–1970s

Now on to your work. When did you actually begin your career as an artist; was it in 1975?
I think so.

The same year that your mother died.
That was, I suppose, in a way coincidental. My youngest child was at primary school and I just had a little bit of time, a little window of opportunity.

Was starting to paint a sudden Yeatsian 'impulse of delight', or was it like a volcano suddenly erupting after smouldering away for many years?
Well, I am not sure it was either of those. I always had a vague idea that I might paint one day but I didn't really know when, and with three children hadn't really had time to think about it.

Having a famous mother as a sculptor and a famous father as a painter, did you ever consider sculpture or was it always going to be painting?
No, definitely not. I think in colour and I dream in colour. So it was always going to be painting.

Would you say you are more or less self-taught, like Alfred Wallis, or did you ever

attend art school or have private lessons?
I would really call myself self-taught. Somebody did persuade me to attend one or two evening art classes near Shepherd's Bush in the late 1950s, but that was largely to make up the numbers for the class. I had a rather inspired teacher who realized immediately that I did *not* like powder paint and she went to the trouble to get me watercolours or maybe it was gouache in tubes, and I did one or two brightly-coloured seascapes and interiors, which I quite enjoyed. I don't like wishy-washy paint at all. After that I got married and had children and we had a very small house and I certainly didn't have any time.

Were your earliest works landscapes or still lifes?
Well, quite honestly, we were living in Leicestershire, which is not a very inspiring county, and as I had a few still-life objects I started with those. My children went to Wreake Valley Comprehensive School, near Leicester, and my husband, Michael, taught human morphology at Nottingham University.

Did you do any paintings of the surrounding countryside?
No, because it is incredibly boring!

Julia, Alison and Jeremy Kidd with their grandmother Barbara Hepworth at her 70th birthday party, St Ives, January 1973

Before you began to paint in 1975 and after, did you and Michael and your three children come to St Ives every year?
Yes, as a family we would come down for a couple of weeks and I suppose what really happened was that I just assimilated the landscape and colours. Subconsciously, really, even as a child.

When did you begin to paint St Ives townscapes and Penwith landscapes?
I am trying to remember just when that was. I think the seascape *Porthmeor*, 1982, was one of the first St Ives pictures. I also painted some seascapes in the Orkneys in 1982 [p.16] and some Derbyshire landscapes in 1984 [p.35]. I am just trying to remember when I first put one or two pictures into the Wills Lane Gallery when Reg Singh was running it, but I think that was only still lifes. I had my first one-man show at the Field Gallery, Farnsfield, Nottinghamshire in 1979. Then Montpelier Studio, as they were called then, wrote to me and said they had seen some work of mine in the Wills Lane and could I bring six paintings for them to see at their gallery in London. They had just started this gallery and I took some work up and they offered me an exhibition in 1980. So that was my first London one-man show.

Dell [Casdagli] told us a story about your father visiting your first exhibition at

Montpelier Studio in 1980 and liking a particular picture and because of that, someone bought it. Did Ben comment on your work? Did he own one of your pictures?
Bernice Sandelson [p.56], the gallery owner, bought *Still Life on Navy Blue*, 1979 [p.8], the one Ben admired. Yes, my father was encouraging and liked one of the first paintings I did in evening class. I think he was pleased about my first one-man show at Montpelier. He didn't own any of my pictures, but of course he lived abroad for many years.

Do you think there were any conscious, key influences on your work early on? Perhaps your father's still lifes, and his Cornish still life/landscape compositions, or the work of William Scott?
I am still a great admirer of William Scott who, sadly, I met only once, briefly. I think, subconsciously, my father was an influence, and probably so was Alfred Wallis, but not consciously.

What about the work of St Ives–born artist Bryan Pearce, whose work your mother encouraged from early in his career? Perhaps it is merely fortuitous, but I have noticed, and several friends have remarked on, the similarities between the relatively unmodulated areas of colour in your landscapes, and unbroken, completely flat colours in Pearce's work.

Derbyshire No.1
(1984)
gouache, 21.5 x 28 cm

Glass with Grey and Green (Mini)
(1985)
gouache, 8.1 x 6 cm
PRIVATE COLLECTION

View from 7 (Mini)
(1989)
gouache, 6.3 x 11.5 cm
PRIVATE COLLECTION

I do not think at all, and my methods are completely different, even though they may appear similar. For example, my way of painting brick walls would be done in exactly the opposite way to him.

I have several questions about your working method. To achieve subtle gradations of colour, do you sometimes rub the paint surface with a cloth, a palette knife or perhaps your finger?
I like to use my fingers to paint and achieve textures, when possible, particularly with oil. I occasionally use a cloth. In oil, I like to build up the surfaces over time; but I also like to paint very fine lines with all my mediums.

Do you sometimes dilute oil paint with turpentine so that it may be applied more thinly?
Yes, sometimes.

In your still-life pictures, do you paint the objects first and then fill in the background colours around them?

It very much depends. Sometimes I can be inspired to paint colours first and then add the objects. Other times I start with the objects. With landscapes and seascapes, I do the drawing first.

In almost all your still lifes there are horizontal, curved bands of colour across the top and bottom of the composition, quite sensuous and gently lyrical. Tell me about this characteristic feature of your work and how it evolved.
I believe this process was subconscious and just developed. It is partly a matter of trying to achieve a balance.

Are there other artists whom you admire... perhaps Chardin and Morandi? Are there half a dozen or so in the history of art, a sort of Desert Island Discs of painters?
Other artists of influence might be Giotto, Cimabue, Fra Angelico, Piero della Francesca. Later, Whistler, Picasso's early work, some Matisse, Modigliani, Miró, Craigie Aitchison and Howard Hodgkin. Oddly enough, I think in recent years Turner has grown on me more

Small Still Life on Red (Mini)
(2005)
gouache, 3.3 x 6.4 cm

Still Life with Decanter (Mini)
(2007)
gouache, 6.5 x 11.5 cm

than he used to. I suppose I like simplicity really.

Did you find your own voice early in your career or did it take a number of years before the unmistakable Rachel Nicholson style emerged?
This question is better answered by an outsider, but I would say probably early on.

As an outsider, I would agree. Describe an ideal working day, with no distractions or interruptions. Do you follow a fairly regular routine, say paint from 10 to 12 or 1 and from 3 to 6, or do you work more when the spirit moves you?
Regular hours are much the best, with spaces in between when the time is right for me.

For me one of the most enchanting aspects of your work is the marriage of landscape with still-life objects in the foreground. In the picture I own, *The Island with Decanter*, 2005–07 [p.139], the decanter, I think you said, belonged to your father [p.13]? Are there half a dozen or so objects

that Ben owned which appear in your pictures from time to time?
Yes, I've got about a dozen. My Ben Nicholson still life objects include: small plate with blue stripes and inner blue spots; hammered pewter mug; ridged decanter; small lustre goblet with gold inside; mug with letters [p.13]; blue flower patterned mug [p.13]; jug with blue stripe [p.25]; large brown jug; large brown mug; mug with feet [p.13]; glass, thick rim; glass, thin rim. Sometimes the more beautiful objects don't work out so well and then occasionally the more unlikely ones work out better for painting.

Your landscapes and townscapes are mainly of the Penwith Peninsula and above all of St Ives: views of the town and its harbour, views seen through windows, Porthmeor Beach and the Atlantic Ocean, with Clodgy Point to the west and The Island to the east. Have you painted many other landscapes in the UK?
Once a year we used to go camping in Derbyshire in the mid-1980s not far from Ashbourne and there is lots of beautiful landscape around there [pp.35 and 79].

Still Life (Mini)
(1995)
gouache, 3.9 x 8.1 cm

Caroline's Mug (Mini)
(2008)
gouache, 3.8 x 4.6 cm

I used to go off drawing and I would take a few photographs as a reference, and then do the paintings afterwards. I have also painted landscapes of the Orkneys, Cumbria, Yorkshire, Nottinghamshire, Sussex, Dorset and the Isles of Scilly.

Do you always begin your landscape and townscape pictures by sketching your subject in pencil *in situ*?
Always.

After the initial, *plein air* drawing has been completed, do you continue to work out of doors with acrylic, or gouache or oil, or is the next stage studio work?
I never paint out of doors. I may work a little on the drawing later in my studio with photographs only as a reference. Then I proceed with the painting. However, I like to complete the St Ives paintings whilst in St Ives. Occasionally I add or alter them later in my London studio.

Do you also begin your still-life subjects by first sketching in pencil?
Yes.

Most of your work is on board rather than canvas. Why is that?

Well, it depends on practicality. I haven't really done many landscapes on canvas. This is partly because it is easier, in a way, if you are going camping and so on, to take board rather than a canvas, more practical, you see. It varies.

The little 'minis' that our friend Dell Casdagli owns, are they on board?
They are all gouache on board.

I gather that the minis are not for sale; they are gifts for family and friends.
Yes.

Well, my next question is about gouache, acrylic and oil. They each have different qualities and, as we were saying, acrylic, if you are down here wanting to take work back to London, dries very quickly. Do you have a preference among oil, acrylic and gouache?
I don't really have a preference, I just think it is a good idea to vary the surface and the mediums because they do different things and you get such different results. But I only paint in oil at home in London because it takes a long time to dry. It's a practical thing too.

Is the ambience of where you are painting important? I mean, is it a very different

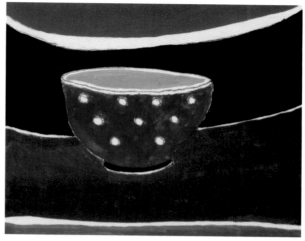

Still Life (Mini)
(1995)
gouache, 3.9 x 8.7 cm

Still Life (Mini)
(1997)
gouache, 5.4 x 6.6 cm

experience painting down here than painting in your studio in London? Or are you totally immersed and it doesn't really much matter?
I suppose it doesn't matter too much. What I most want is a nice, quiet, peaceful atmosphere (laughs) and to immerse myself in music.

Does the intense summer light affect your work if you are painting in St Ives in June, July and August? Is that reflected in the painting itself?
I think it does. One of the aspects anyhow is that if you come in the summer, you get that much more time for actually painting, because on a good day I can paint until 9 o'clock at night.

But is the light in the painting itself much brighter?
Certainly the colours are affected by the light and so vary accordingly, although in St Ives it can almost be too bright, oddly enough. Very, very bright. But I do find it a great help to have good weather as there is a lot more clarity. I think my paintings probably have reflected the weather, in the sense that if I am doing a seascape or some still lifes and if the sea is very bright blue, then the picture will be very bright blue,

but if it's a much quieter, softer, paler colour, then that would be reflected in my picture.

There are no human figures in your work and somehow I feel they don't really belong.
No, I suppose for some reason I have never really felt the inclination. I have probably done one or two, not more. I would sometimes love to but I don't have the confidence to do figures. I have seen one or two wonderful-looking people, usually with a dark skin and wearing some fantastic clothes and thinking 'gosh, wouldn't it be marvellous to do that.' I do remember being influenced by the colour of a man's green shirt and a white tie with spots, which translated into one of my earliest still-life pictures, which I still own. It has a green background and a spotted jug [p.11]. I think those colours really emanated from seeing this person in the clothes he was wearing. But at the same time, I find that in some ways music is more important to me than painting, in the sense that painting is almost part of my life, and I have been brought up with it and it has always been around me, whereas I suppose music was something that I discovered on my own and I can't really do without. In fact, as a child, I used to sit on the stairs outside my mother's studio and

Alan's Mini
(2008)
gouache, 6.3 x 10.1 cm
ALAN WILKINSON

Dell's Mini
(1985)
gouache, 5.7 x 10.1 cm
DELL CASDAGLI

listen to her playing gramophone records, which I thought was wonderful. Furthermore, I work to music.

Who are your favourite composers?
Mostly those of the Baroque period, such as Bach, Vivaldi, Telemann and Handel, especially Bach and Handel. Classical period: Haydn, Beethoven, and especially Mozart and Schubert and in particular his songs. Mozart has been a firm favourite since the age of eleven. Listening to music whilst working gives me ideas, gives me colours and a sense of peace, which I am always trying to achieve in my work.

How very interesting. I had no idea that music has played such an important part in your life. Do you think over the thirty years or so your style and colour have changed greatly, or the subject matter?
I think it is easier for the outsider to see whether they think that has happened, but perhaps now the colours are more muted.

New subjects. What about the views of St Ives through windows: from the Tate St Ives restaurant, from Barnaloft, and from the houses and flats of friends. Is that a fairly recent motif, or have you done such views for some time?
Well, I am really trying to remember when that started. Originally I think I just did

seascapes and then gradually the still life started to come into my pictures. I had certainly started incorporating still-life objects in landscapes in 1984. In paintings of St Ives with part exterior, part interior, I should perhaps mention *Island with Spotty Jug*, 1994 [right]. This was exhibited at Tate St Ives in 1995 in an exhibition called 'Porthmeor Beach: A Century of Images'. Later, Michael Tooby, then curator of Tate St Ives, invited me to participate in an exhibition in 1998/99 reflecting the connections between Dartington, Leeds, Corsham and St Ives. He particularly asked me to paint views from the Tate restaurant [pp.23, 110, 111 and 117]. These were part interior/exterior and, if I remember correctly, four of these were included along with nine other works.

You are the third generation of Nicholson artists and your son Jeremy Kidd is the fourth. At what age did he begin his career, where did he study, and can you describe what sort of work he does? Is there any connection with your work, that of his grandparents Ben Nicholson and Barbara Hepworth, or his great-grandfather, William Nicholson?
In 1980, at the age of eighteen, Jeremy began his training at De Montfort University, Leicester, specializing in sculpture. He is an artist who has lived in Los Angeles since 1987. He employs the camera as his medium,

Porthmeor Beach and the Island

Island with Spotty Jug
(1994)
acrylic, 30.5 x 40.6 cm

Rachel with *View from 18 with Cups*, c.1988

and explores a fantastic or fictional reality created by reinterpreting his cityscape photographs. Using the computer, he edits and adapts multiple images expressing visceral urban views that lie somewhere between memory and observation. This is driven by his experience of the dramatic monoliths and canyons of the American landscape. He showed an interest in still life in his early work, a theme inherited from the Nicholsons. His love of sculpture derives from his grandmother. He believes that his innate compositional abilities are inherited, but also acquired through exposure to Ben Nicholson's and Barbara Hepworth's work that surrounded him as he grew up.

In August of this year [2008], you have lived in and spent holidays in Carbis Bay and St Ives for seventy years. Do you still feel the excitement, as I do after a mere thirty-five years of sporadic visits, when you arrive by car or train and see St Ives

Bay with Virginia Woolf's Godrevy lighthouse in the distance, and then the town of St Ives, its harbour and The Island, and finally from your Barnaloft flat, Porthmeor Beach and the, at times, mighty Atlantic Ocean?
Well, all of that. If you come into the town from Carbis Bay and around the bend at the top, there is this amazing bright blue sea with the bay and Godrevy lighthouse. If you are leaving the town, there is another memorable view of Clodgy Point, Porthmeor Beach and The Island. This is especially so on a fine day. Certainly if you come into this flat (18 Barnaloft) at high tide it is stunning because you feel, well, almost at one with the sea.

One feels as if one is on board ship.
Yes, it's wonderful.

A year or so ago, you may remember, I wrote to you and quoted Herbert Read's famous phrase 'the geometry of fear', a term which he used to describe the sculpture of Adams, Armitage Butler, Chadwick, Clarke, Meadows, Paolozzi and Turnbull, whose work was rather spiky and menacing. Borrowing three words from Read and adding to them, I wrote that for me your work embodies 'the geometry of fear, and tranquillity'. Do you think that is an apt description?
I think it's a very good description. Interestingly enough, the thing I feel very often when I go into a room of my mother's sculptures, or even the other day when I was in the St Ives library, is that her sculptures often give me this feeling of peace, so maybe we were both looking for the same thing.

Critical views

RELATIVES CAN BE INTIMIDATING. On Rachel Nicholson's own admission the reputation of her parents Barbara Hepworth and Ben Nicholson inhibited her desire to practise painting (or music, her other passion).

Rachel Nicholson therefore never trained as a painter though as the third generation of a line of professional artists she could hardly escape the influence of the studio. However she considers her career started in 1975 when she inherited some painting equipment from her mother.

A cursory view of this exhibition will reveal that the family inheritance was more profound than that. The images of mugs and jugs, the division within the picture into rectangles and linear strips, and the texture of the paint itself owe a great deal to the work of her father in particular. Indeed some of the favourite objects in her studio are the very same mugs and plates that belonged to Ben Nicholson himself.

The reason for drawing attention to this is to identify the special talent of Rachel Nicholson, her sensitivity to colour, and her tender obsession with familiar objects which provide a constant stimulus to explore a private world which she shares with us in these canvases.

Judging by one or two of the larger paintings there are signs that she may be moving towards a more dramatic style and we can anticipate developments.

David Hughes

(organiser, arts education, Leicestershire)
Exhibition card for first London show at
Montpelier Studio, 1980

RACHEL NICHOLSON (ONE OF THE triplets born to Ben Nicholson and Barbara in 1934) was the daughter of a sculptor; this shows in her work, which with formal spareness and economy, highlights an interest in the pure shape of simple objects like domestic ceramics or silverware. She develops her father's interest in the facets and flattened shapes of cups, saucers, spoons or mugs. She also introduces venetian red highlights, and is sensitive to the decorative significance of pattern as contributing not only to the vitality of secondary pictorial imagery but also as a pleasing visual sensation in its own right. Again like her father, she gives a black rim to the curves of these objects, throwing them into illusory relief. Her palette is restricted to beige, grey and blue but her landscape view of St Ives Bay, *Pig 'n' Fish* [1992], reveals she can use blue with a versatility to express fully the atmosphere of a place. Her landscapes tend to focus on a distant headland or expanse of sea as viewed beyond foreground rooftop architecture. During the 1980s and beyond, this contemplative and accomplished painter has exhibited on a regular basis at the Montpelier Studio in London, proving alongside artists like Anne Rothenstein, John Hitchens, Freddie Gore, Lucien Pissarro and many others that it is possible to paint with an authentic voice even within the shadow of a giant parental tree.

Peter Davies

From *St Ives Revisited*, Old Bakehouse
Publications, 1994

RACHEL NICHOLSON'S PAINTINGS have an instant accessibility and charm; they draw you into a vision of St Ives and the landscape around it, seen in a rapt attention that few people can retain beyond childhood. The freshness of her view is powerful enough to survive prolonged encounter with her work; the simplicity is chimerical at once genuine and deceptive. The commonplace domestic objects, for example, ranged in the foreground of many of her canvases have been rendered abstract by their mysterious scatter in relation to each other, and by their use to define the floating angles of sills and tables giving on to high windows and balconies from which the scenes are viewed. Suddenly, strangely important, they invite us to look both at them and beyond them, in a marriage of still life and landscape. The geometries of roofscape, 'drawn' as well as painted, the gently skewed perspectives, the areas of flat colour in a muted palette, and the distances framed in windows, are playfully allusive and give Rachel Nicholson's art a fascinating dimension, representing St Ives in the light of the present, but also as a historical subject of art, the locus of the vision of other painters before her. In reflecting, containing and enhancing a tradition like that of St Ives without losing the sense of instantaneity – the sense of each painting as freshly seen – Rachel Nicholson continues to offer images which are at once highly idiosyncratic, and deeply learned, the product of an unjaded vision and a loving eye.

Jill Paton Walsh

Rachel Nicholson (exhibition catalogue)
Montpelier Sandelson, 1997

AS A LANDSCAPE PAINTER RACHEL Nicholson must be counted one of the direct inheritors of the modern, English idiom of the 1920s and 1930s. She is also a painter of rhythmically beautiful still lifes. Like the pioneers of the Modern Movement, among them her father, Ben Nicholson, Winifred Nicholson, Paul Nash, and Christopher Wood, she often fuses the two subjects. It is this device, bringing still life into her landscapes, which she continues to take in new and imaginative directions. Her particular combination of formal simplicity and decorative interest, topographical detail and the slightly surreal surprise of finding teacups by the wayside, accounts for the immediate appeal of her pictures to a late 20th- and early 21st-century public.

Although she taught herself to paint relatively late, in 1975, within years her presence in mixed exhibitions won an appreciative audience. Her first solo show in Nottinghamshire in 1979 launched a flourishing independent career. She has been working professionally now for nearly thirty years, developing a personal and very recognizable style inspired by that generation of early English modernists, of which both her parents, Barbara Hepworth and Ben Nicholson, were key movers. Their example, their aesthetic ideas and European influences, were the bedrock of her informal education. The unschooled imagination of the Cornish landscape artist Alfred Wallis provided a further spur, as did her admiration for

Porthmeor with Fishing Boat
(2004)
acrylic, 22.9 x 29.7 cm

the sparse still-life compositions of William Scott, a regular visitor to St Ives, where she grew up.

When Rachel Nicholson started painting in 1975 it was to still-life compositions that she turned first. At the time, her working space was the small attic of her Leicestershire home. As wife and mother her arena was restricted, and of necessity she chose her subject matter from what was at hand. From early childhood, she has been obsessed by objects and their meticulous arrangement in relation to each other and to their surroundings. She knew instantly, to her sister's surprise, when something had been moved. Like her father, she has an instinctive eye for placing things on a shelf or table according to shape and colour. Her first painting subjects were chosen from the assembly of jugs, mugs and other objects in her home, including two ceramic pots given her by her father. Since then, her collection has grown considerably with the acquisition of objects, or gifts from friends. Her studio now has the panoramic look of an interior landscape lovingly studded with glass, metal and ceramic, as well as numerous bone spoons, a favourite motif for giving linear structure to her spatial compositions. Nicholson's earliest still-life work, painted thickly in gouache, has a raw-edged spontaneity and freedom about it, which, she acknowledges, was therapeutic. 'I was trying to achieve a sense of peace,' she says. A few years later, she was free to get out into the landscape, painting the wider aspects of rural Derbyshire, and then increasingly the Cornish landscape. She has known Cornwall since childhood, and its rugged contours particularly in and around St Ives, where she has a flat, have immense appeal for her.

The interplay between the two central themes in her work, still life and landscape, is explored for the first time in Rachel Nicholson's perceptive layout of this catalogue. The double-page spreads juxtapose the two, highlighting their thematic similarities. Pure landscapes, such as *Towards Rottingdean*, 2005, are now relatively rare in her work, and more often replaced by landscapes and townscapes incorporating elements of the still lifes, which feature independently in facing plates. Compare, for instance, *Porthmeor with Fishing Boat* [p.45] and *Sextet*: the organic lines and colours in the still life find an attractive echo in the undulating landscape. St Ives, the dominant subject of these new paintings, is a small town of densely packed houses, a beach, harbour, and pier, embraced by a sweeping coast with distant promontory and islets. But her interest is more than scenic, always implying the life of the town and its on-looking inhabitants. Exploiting a visual strategy used by Ben Nicholson, Christopher Wood and others in the 1920s and 1930s, her views are sometimes framed in a window, its sill laid out with ornaments, which find their harmonious counterpart in the landscape beyond. Pushing the device further, she merges the intriguing lines of a window overhang with the geometry of the buildings beyond. At other times, she extends the view inwards, to where in *Another View from Joseph's* [p.115], a free-standing table replaces the sill. Then, in *A Barnaloft Flat* [p.122], the landscape forms a distant continuity with a spacious interior. The distinction between interior and exterior vanishes completely in some of her most characteristic compositions, such as *Godrevy with Spotty Cup* [p.125] and *Near Eagles Nest* [p.19]. There is a delightful sense of humour in these pictures, in which still life makes a deceptively casual appearance in the landscape.

Although Nicholson received no formal art education and little encouragement at home, her upbringing in an artistic milieu in which both parents worked professionally helped to train her eye by example. Her concerns were and remain those of the early British modernists: her devotion to still life and landscape, her formal interests in compositional geometry, in rhythmic line, pattern, and the value of colour, and her belief in the fresh, untrained, or naïve, eye. Her search, as she says, 'for some sort of perfection, for a balance or harmony in my work' reflects the ideals of a generation which inspired her own ideas. The close connection between still life and landscape substantiates this aim. It lies at the heart of her work, and distinguishes a consistent and personal vision, which she continues to expand and refine.

Judith Bumpus
(art historian)
'Still Life into Landscape: Rachel Nicholson – New Paintings', Caroline Wiseman Modern Art, 2006

Appreciations

FIFTEEN YEARS AGO RACHEL Nicholson asked if she could come to our flat in St Ives to draw. The painting that ensued, *View from the Saltings*, 1994 [p.21], is one of our most treasured possessions. It hangs over our St Ives work table where we are inspired not only by the view but by Rachel's reordering of it.

The thinnest of barriers between inside and out is transparent and formal, creating a Mondrian-like composition. The open balcony door leads in an instant to Clodgy Point. It is early morning and a summons to go out, to look for seals and wild flowers, to start the coastal walk to Zennor. All is possible, even probable, in this world of light and space. The wide sky and sea are untroubled, uncomplicated; everything has a place and is in place. It is a good day for living in an ordered world. Chaos there may be but it is elsewhere. When we try to analyse why we like the painting so much, we resort to a non-analytical phrase: life-enhancing.

In all of Rachel's landscapes there seems to be the mystery of order. Rocks, boats, trees, posts, fields, houses are as precisely arranged as all those jugs, mugs, pots and spoons. Precise, but fluid. Fields are arranged rhythmically; puddles are balanced; abstract patterns repeated with variations. Above all the seeing eye has a twinkle. The observer is quite human.

The colour and shape of the landscape are echoed in the still-life canvases: granite, foam, slate, flat blue. The sea is never far away. Rachel's work is, for us, an invitation to share a passion. The spirit and shape of Cornwall are mighty currents which lose nothing by understatement.

Resonances abound, including Barbara Hepworth's:

'Nothing we ever touch and feel or see and love is ever lost to us. From birth to old age it is retained like the warmth of rocks, the coolness of grass and the everflow of the sea.'
Clare and Eric Ash
Friends

MY CONNECTION WITH RACHEL is multi-faceted. Like her I spent my childhood in Cornwall, and throughout most of my adult life I have been closely involved with her mother's sculpture and drawings, and the work of painters from St Ives has been an important thread in the New Art Centre's history. All this has made me appreciate Rachel's paintings and admire their quiet and poetic serenity. She herself is a gentle and private person who has responded to all the strands of her background in a remarkable way.

Perhaps this quotation from Wordsworth used by David Baxandall about Ben Nicholson's work could apply equally to his daughter's paintings:

'While with an eye made quiet by the power / Of harmony, and the deep power of joy, / We see into the life of things.'
Madeleine Bessborough
New Art Centre, Roche Court, Salisbury

MY FISHERMAN'S COTTAGE IN St Ives is at the other end of Back Road from the cottage where Alfred Wallis once lived. Rachel asked me soon after we first met if she could do some drawings of the harbour from my window, and this work grew into a series of paintings of my 'room with a view' through Rachel's eyes. Rachel, by now a very good friend, gave me one of the paintings, *Slantways 2*, 2004 (p.22), in exchange for what I regarded as rather meagre architectural advice; an unequal piece of bartering very much in my favour.

I see Rachel's work as continuing a tradition very strong in the history of art in St Ives; the theme, 'trope' as critics would call it, favoured by Ben Nicholson, Christopher Wood, Bryan Pearce and others, whereby a still-life group on a window sill is set against the landscape beyond. The balance and relationship between the still life and landscape are subject to much variation: In Christopher Wood's *Anemones in a Cornish Window*, 1930, the jug of flowers is the centred, realistically-painted subject, with a blowing brown curtain, and a beached brown boat beyond, scarcely smaller or less important than the jug in the foreground. Seventeen years later, in Ben Nicholson's *11 November 1947 (Mousehole)*, the still-life element is a self-contained abstract, Cubist composition of bottles and mugs in the foreground, set against a landscape, the whole bound together with a uniform texture within a single pictorial plane [see related work, p.10].

Rachel's concerns are close to those of the early British Modernists, both in subject matter and formal approach. Still life and landscape and their close connection are at the heart of her work, and she continues to develop and refine the theme with great originality.

In my painting, *Slantways 2*, Rachel extends the view of the harbour inwards, a small table replacing the sill. I was aware of her personal taste in the lovely collection of domestic objects that fill her studio and feature in her paintings, and was concerned that she might not be happy to work with my own possessions, and would feel the need to import some of her own into the composition. However, once she had exclaimed with pleasure at my black and white spotted tea towel, and had moved certain items upstairs from my kitchen, all seemed well. Only the wooden chair is not mine.

I spend a long time looking at this painting in my London house, so far from the sea. I think that Rachel does something very inventive with the window theme that I had not perceived before in her work. The window to the view is painted here in such a way that it becomes, or can be seen as, a frame to a seascape 'picture' on the wall. (A suggestion of mitred corners remains in the drawing.) This painting-within-a painting now becomes an object, a 'still-life' object furnishing a windowless room; a very clever paradox.

Fenella Clemens
Photographer

VIEW FROM THE BACK OF ST IVES
[p.52]

A place, the essence of that place.
Familiar and loved Porthmeor.
A view, loaded with a lifetime of memories
so delicately portrayed, the most known,
    a notion.

A unique Artist's perspective, frozen,
the vehicle for my nostalgia, changing.
My metronome of memories through
    a lifetime.

A walk. A run.
Friends and family.
    A childhood remembered.
Crashing waves, moving sand and
    eroding cliffs.
My nostalgia, captured.

Elantha Evans
Friend and architect

I CAUGHT A BRIEF GLIMPSE OF THIS
painting [right] on my way through Rachel's
studio. I was stunned. On my way back, I
paused to look and immediately wanted it.

It's a wonderfully balanced composition
– a painting within a painting, delicately
painted in whites, greys and pale hues.

The interior and exterior are one; the
inside leading out to the town and landscape.
The two worlds flow into one another on a
glorious summer's day.

The single-point perspective dominates
the interior space with the foreground laid
out in an L-shape displaying the five set

pieces – a spoon, jar, bowl, mug and ball
– all in accented tones, photographically
executed.

The diagonal of the interior continues
outwards terminating in a chimney. This
divides the foreground into the harbour
(blue) and roof (grey), with a continuous
hinterland beyond running the width of
the picture. On the opposite side, an open
window leads the eye to the blue harbour.
Accented verticals of balustrades and
fenestration frame the randomness of
the dwelling and landscape.

It is all man-made. Are the five precious
objects more valued, more special, more
permanent than the view? Is the exterior
more permanent, or does it have the same
fragility? Does the outside view capture a
nostalgia for times past, or is it a frozen
moment before unwanted change?

It is a beautiful painting which plays with
opposites, contradictions and exaggerations.
It captures the essence of the place – its light.

Eldred Evans
Friend and architect

RACHEL'S WORK HAS PUNCTUATED
events in my life since the late 1970s, with
acquisitions and, occasionally, delightful
surprises. Sometimes minute paintings
have been delivered to mark a special
birthday or house move. They are treasured.

We bought a painting in 1979 from
Rachel's first solo exhibition, which was at
the Field Gallery, Farnsfield, Nottinghamshire.
Her still-life subjects were often familiar,

View towards the Harbour
(2004)
acrylic, 24.8 x 29.9 cm

View from the Back of St Ives
(2004/05)
acrylic, 39.9 x 50.8 cm

ELANTHA EVANS

but one at this exhibition made us laugh. *Still Life with Fox*, 1978 [p.54], shows a careful arrangement of tableware. The little fox gave another dimension, if not animation, to the painting.

In all Rachel's work there is great clarity, but I imagine sometimes there is a feeling that Cornwall, land- or seascapes, is her inheritance and this is demonstrated in the wavy lines, an abstracted form of tide on shore, upon which her compositions of cups and milk jugs lurch slightly.

We were invited to St Ives for a holiday and were so delighted with the unbeatable views, that, when Bernard Leach's Barnaloft flat came on the market, we bought it in 1981. We retained many of the attractive features that Leach had commissioned from the architect: white kitchen dresser and cupboards, with black Formica surfaces. I added red mugs and cutlery. 'All I need now,' I said, 'is a red colander.' Rachel's solution was to paint in miniature a pan, a kitchen knife and the red colander. *Still Life with Colander*, 1981 [p.82] hangs now in the kitchen in St Ives.
Andrea Frears
Friend

RACHEL MADE US A BEAUTIFUL pocket-sized painting as a wedding present. On Porthmeor beach, a minute seagull appears to be having a stand-off with two jugs on a table top in the foreground. The painting has the quiet balance you would expect from her work but is also hilarious.

She has created a completely believable world which appears to be cool, straightforward and poised.

Rachel might seem to be a little shy and serious if you didn't know her but is in fact a person with a naughty twinkle in her eye. She is a great and modest painter who works in almost laboratory conditions, she's funny and sharp, gives fantastic conspiratorial winks, worries about the weather and starts phone calls with 'The trouble is…'
Naomi Frears
Artist and friend

THE INFINITE BREADTH OF TONAL PALETTE AND OBJECT
My mother places a special value on her chosen objects of veneration as she features them in her paintings. The appreciation and desire for such objects were most likely acquired because she grew up surrounded by the sculptures of Barbara Hepworth and the still lifes featured in Ben Nicholson's paintings. Indeed, she inherited from Ben some of these beautiful still-life objects that appear in her paintings. In addition, she has added many new ones to the collection and has also been given additional cups and objects by friends and family. If we are very lucky, some of these new members of her collection will also make it into her compositions.

These carefully selected and arranged objects of appreciation are strategically placed around her studio and acquire a heightened iconographic status. Every object is carefully considered in relation

Still Life with Fox
(1978)
oil, 31.7 x 36.2 cm

to the next one in her home, as they are in her studio, long before reaching her canvas.

I'm not quite sure if the selected, idiosyncratic domestic objects are watching the worn British landscape or the viewer. In the still lifes, often sitting mid-ground on a horizontal band of built up, painted, texture Rachel's humble objects embody a gentle but whimsical character. They are the first place the eye falls and for me represent people or a small family of distinct characters. They also provide a counterpoint for the landscape to exist, which appears to be seen through their eyes but from the safe vantage point of a domestic plateau. In turn we view the still lifes, on their flowing swathes of muted hues, from our external vantage point.

I believe the artist is forced to develop a special relationship with what is painted and perhaps for my mother they become invested with intention and spirit and therefore character. I have also noticed that the portraits of a portrait painter often resemble to some degree the artist who painted them. And it is for this reason I feel that my mother's objects are reflections or projections of something of her character and perhaps desire for family.

There is an exquisite tonal range and balance of colours that is exclusive to northern Europe and England. This of course has as much as anything to do with the quality of light that forces the English painter to observe the more subtle range of tone and hue; for that is often all that is available. Rachel does this particularly well. Over the years I have seen an infinite range and amalgamation of tones and subtle colours in her work that few other artists have achieved.

There is a great depth to the way the English use their language that may have been encouraged by the awful weather and lack of light. And having been asked by Rachel, while living in the United States, to send her as many different tubes of grey acrylics as I can find, bears out what might be construed as an obsession with infinite tonal variance. This breadth of tonal palette serves in her development of a sophisticated painterly language, which seems more related to the exploratory vocation of an abstract painter than a conventional landscape or still life artist. And here intersect her concerns for advancing the language of painting and her very personal relationship with cups and other prized objects.

Jeremy Kidd
Artist

RACHEL NICHOLSON CREATES A backwater of calm in the hurly-burly of the twenty-first century. Her work memorialises the enduring artistic legacy of an Edwardian grandfather, modernist parents, and a childhood in St Ives, a town to which she has frequently returned. Her roots are permanently present. Her shadowless paintings are cut off from the anxieties of present day conflicts and celebrate the safe haven of tea time by the sea. How we all long for that!

Jeremy Lewison
Art historian

MY WIFE CAITLIN AND I BOTH LOVE the sea, having spent lots of our childhoods in different parts of the world by the sea. Our Rachel Nicholson *Towards the Island*, 2006 [p.134], is a reminder in some ways of somewhere we would like to go back to or head towards in the future. Godrevy lighthouse in the distance snags the eye and hints at the distance and challenge ahead to reach the goal but the presence of the spotted tea cup and saucer and the sugar bowl in the foreground provides a comforting feeling that the journey does not necessarily have to be too harsh...

The picture is a calming one in subject matter and colour and we keep it in the hall so that when we come back from a busy office or frenzied school day it speaks of quietness, space and a sense of contentment far away from everyday London. At the least, it is a simple daily pleasure and, at the most, may be it makes us better, calmer parents and people every day.

Robin Osmond
Businessman

WE ARE PROUD TO HAVE GIVEN several exhibitions of Rachel Nicholson's work between 1980 and 2000. Largely self-taught, it was apparent that Rachel was a natural artist who was profoundly influenced by her father's paintings, both in subject matter and style. Indeed, Ben Nicholson turned up one day unannounced at her first exhibition and said, 'I had never realised she could paint so well. I would

have been happy to have painted that one myself' – pointing at a Rachel still life [*Still Life on Navy Blue*, 1979, p.8]. Her sense of colour, and line, however, are distinctly her own and she soon attracted a large and growing band of admirers amongst the public at large.

Bernice Sandelson
Art dealer

RACHEL BRINGS US INTO A WORLD without shadows or clouds or people and allows us to feel through the quiet elegance of the compositions a magnetic alignment with the landscape. Yet the expression of human relationship is present in a magical way because of the absence of any human form. The carefully placed domestic objects enter and observe the landscape but also convey a longing for the attentive intimacy that seems to have just left the scene.

In the still-life paintings, the objects feel like characters in a play, finely choreographed in truth and tension, some sensuous and open, while others are estranged and turn their uncommunicative backs to each other. In *Two Patterned Mugs*, 2004 [p.57], the objects court comfortably with decorative compatibility, light-hearted patterns in happy dialogue.

A meditative calm pervades both landscapes and still lifes and together they draw us into the treasures of Rachel's life-long dialogue with St Ives. In that way the paintings resonate for me with the words of W.H. Auden, in his poem 'New Year Letter':

Two Patterned Mugs
(2004)
acrylic, 39.9 x 50.8 cm

'For art had set in order sense / And feeling and intelligence, / And from its ideal order grew / Our local understanding too.'
Katherine Smalley
Allied Capital Corporation

I AM THE PROUD AND APPRECIATIVE possessor of *Summer Seascape*, 1998 [p.59], and *Spotty Mug on Black and Green*, 2001 [p.129]. Each is typical of Rachel Nicholson's later work. I find an amazing simplicity and tranquillity in both. They hang in different rooms in our house in the Berkshire countryside. We are far from the sea yet all of us who use the house feel very connected to it. Rachel's work keeps us spiritually connected. She has a sturdy assurance in her still lifes and people who glimpse the *Spotty Mug* for the first time are always struck by it. Her inescapably St Ives *Summer Seascape* is a kind of still life of this sublime spot in which light gathers to provide that very special uplift that characterises St Ives. I only get to the house at irregular weekends but Rachel Nicholson's powerful simplicity is one of the key aesthetic signals that I am back home again.
Jon Snow
Newscaster, Channel 4 News

THE FIRST PAINTING I SAW OF Rachel Nicholson's was called *A Nicholson Jug,* 1992. The title tackled head-on the pressure of her illustrious forebears and deftly flicked away any cynical assumptions that might have attended her work. I like to think there was an ambiguity in her title: that it both recognised the legacy of her father, Ben, and grandfather William, both renowned for their paintings of jugs, and claimed the subject for herself.

Ambiguity, it seems to me, is at the heart of Rachel's work. On the one hand, the paintings suggest an innocence of vision: they appear to be simple and evocative descriptions of objects and places. These are objects and places that can be evoked with such simplicity because of the painter's deep familiarity with them: jugs, cups and landscapes she has known all her life. On first sight, indeed, one might mistake them for the work of what has been called a 'naïve artist'.

On the other hand, there is this sense of irony, this knowing recognition of the complex layers of meaning that must attend even such apparently simple works of art. *A Nicholson Jug* acknowledged what many people might be thinking on seeing yet another painter called Nicholson painting that same vessel.

Rachel admits the artificiality of her subjects by exaggerating their oddness. So the familiar motif of a still life before a landscape is given an awkward precision by being situated in the landscape itself — the objects being arrayed on a table which appears to have been abandoned on the beach or at the roadside. Her appreciation of the complex meanings that might be read into such apparently innocent paintings is, for me, signalled by

Summer Seascape
(1998)
acrylic, 25.5 x 35.6 cm
JON SNOW

a series of still lifes painted in the elevated café of Tate St Ives. For those interested in ideas of art and place, there can be few subjects more stimulating than a Nicholson jug set against the Tate's panoramic view of the artists' colony of St Ives over which her parents so famously presided.

But of course, the ultimate irony is that all that complexity of history and meaning is belied by the paintings themselves. They retain a simple freshness, idiosyncrasy and evocative charm that cannot be avoided. The paintings of views capture something of those places. The still lifes similarly catch the essence of the individual objects while their arrangement has a slight awkwardness, as if each is embarrassed in the company of the others. It's that hint of unease that prevents the innocent charms of the paintings from becoming twee and makes them right. Rachel Nicholson appears to paint simply what she has in front of her and which she knows so well. That one can find such nuances in that most basic of artistic endeavours is testament to the depth and subtlety of her achievement.

Chris Stephens
Curator, Modern British Art, Tate Britain

I FIRST FELT I GOT TO KNOW RACHEL Nicholson's work when I was working at Tate St Ives, in the mid-1990s. She visited regularly, at times when the gallery was closed. This was to allow her to spend periods of quiet working time, a request which she gently raised one day but which became quite regular.

My first impression had been that she wished to use the views from the restaurant to inspire subjects [pp.23, 110, 111 and 117]. As is now evident, this was not in fact her primary subject. She soon began to complete paintings that were actually studies of space and light, the architecture of the empty gallery restaurant as an enclosed space, punctuated by views of the townscape and seascape.

The emptiness of the interior space, paradoxically, became an intrinsic part of the meaning of this continuing body of work. The restaurant is, by nature and design, a meeting place, a place of refreshment, somewhere to feast upon the views, the light, the changing weather. At busy times it can ring with noise, and even at the quietest times it echoes with conversation of staff and the sound of work going on.

Rachel Nicholson's paintings are declaratory of silence. Consider meanwhile the evidence of the people passing through. A chair moved into a corner; a mug and a knife: a stillness as if the human touch has left its gentle trace, a fragment of a life passed by.

In recent exhibitions, the accompanying catalogues and graphics have allowed us to glimpse the artist in a corner of her studio. A shelf of mugs and glasses is revealed in the background. The slightest acquaintance with her biography tells us how loaded with memory and association this shelf of mugs and glasses must be. It is as if she is remaking for herself her father's depiction of her grandfather's collection of objects for still lifes.

It has been commented upon with frequency that Ben Nicholson reconsidered his father's still lifes, using the same mugs and glasses – the very same – to completely reinvent the form and content of the still life. One device was the use of the still life in the window, allowing a play between deep space and near space, solid form and the exterior and interior light.

Over the last decade Rachel Nicholson has also continued to make images of the landscape. Many are of the places around Penwith made familiar through the work of her parents, and their artist colleagues of the next generation. Her images retain a lightness of touch and clarity of atmosphere. Some have still lifes in the foreground. A consistent device is to deploy the composition so that it folds around the edge of the painting, using limbs of headland around beaches or enfolding harbour walls to enclose the space within the scene. This sense of enfolding space, curiously, echoes the way that the abstracted backgrounds of her miniature studies of individual objects – jugs, cups, bowls – curve in inversions of the foregrounded object.

In Rachel Nicholson's vision, then, isolated objects speak of the traces of human presence. Respecting the way William Scott's domestic objects quietly fuse the personal, the private and the formal, in her work the discovery of a lonely fork or a waiting table setting brings the sense of impending or passing human contact. At the same time, her landscapes are as if the scenes of cliff, beach, harbour or hamlet are evacuated of resident or visitor.

She does not allow us to think of this quiet, this stillness, as melancholy. Indeed, a comment frequently made of her work is that it has a wry wit; and one might even identify a sense of fun in some of the juxtapositions of charming decoration on pots with carefully managed scenes of town and landscape. Instead, the consistency of her work suggests someone who finds a sense of peace and repose in understanding the visual order of the world around her.

Michael Tooby
Director, Learning and Programmes for the National Museums of Wales

THE WORK OF MANY EMINENT British artists – Ben Nicholson, Terry Frost, Patrick Heron, Lucian Freud, Howard Hodgkin, and David Hockney – to name but a few, hang here, on the walls of our house in London. Rachel Nicholson's work is here too and her paintings are as fresh and vibrant as any of these. Hers seem quiet, yet they are not quiet, they are as powerful in their directness as the best of them. When you are self-taught like Rachel, you have nothing but you and your vision and she succeeds every time.

Caroline Wiseman
Caroline Wiseman Modern and Contemporary, London

The plates

Composition with Two Brown Objects
(1976)
oil, 30.5 x 36.8 cm

Striped Jug, Glass and Black Fork
(1977)
gouache, 29.3 x 34.3 cm

Still Life with Red Stripe on Grey
(1977)
gouache, 28 x 35.2 cm

Jug and Cup on Yellow
(1978)
oil, 32.4 x 38.1 cm

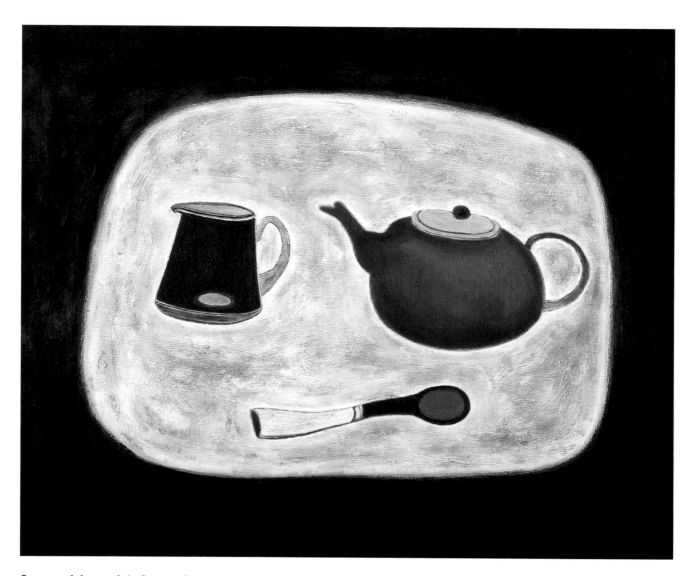

Composition with Stone Colours
(1980)
oil, 26.7 x 34.3 cm
CHILWELL COMPRESSIVE SCHOOL, NOTTINGHAM

Striped Mug on Blues
(1979)
oil, 30.5 x 26.7 cm

Grey Glass, White Jug
(1979)
oil, 26.5 x 31.6 cm

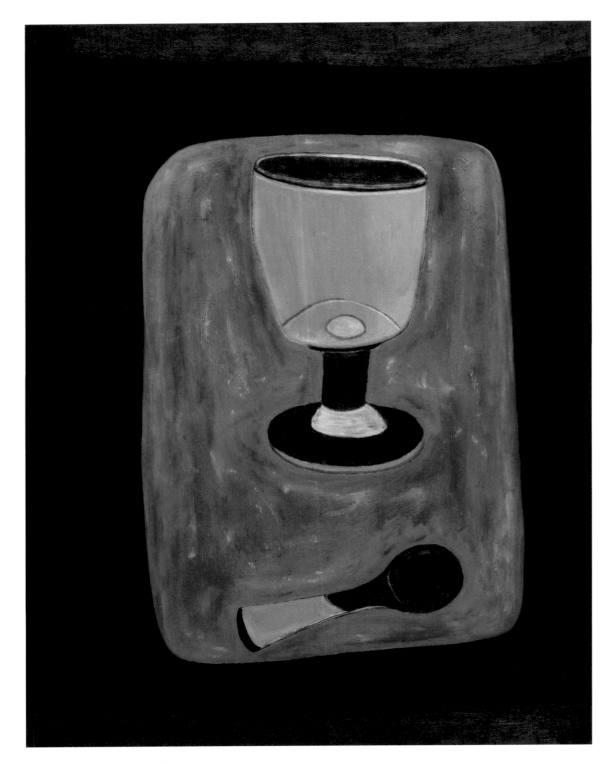

Glass and Spoon on Brown and Grey
(1979)
oil, 34.3 x 26.1 cm

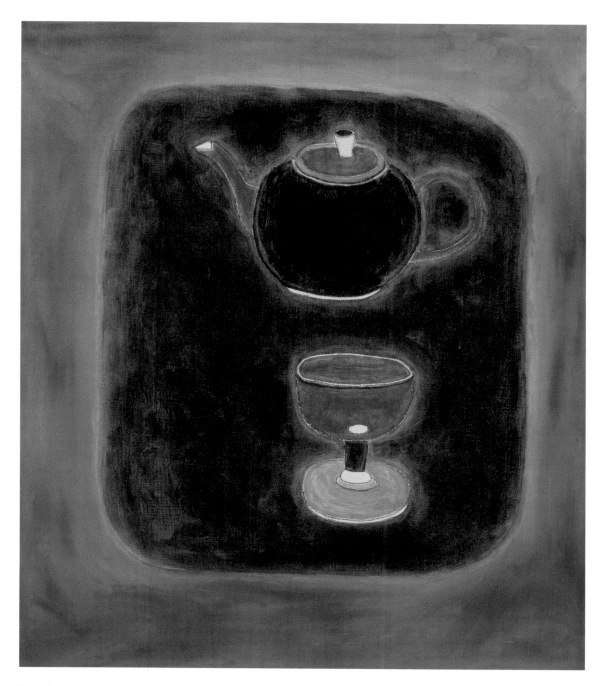

Tea Pot and Glass on Yellow
(1980)
oil, 31.7 x 26.7 cm

Brown and Grey Coffee Jug
(1981)
oil, 29.3 x 25.5 cm

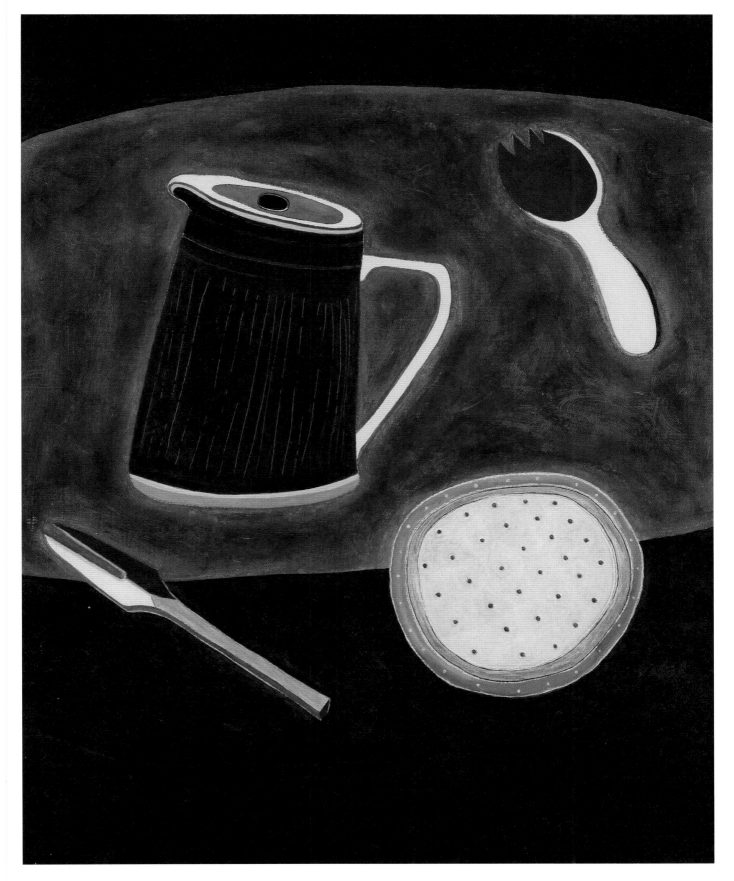

Composition with Black Coffee Jug on Green
(1980)
oil, 37.5 x 30 cm

Goblet with Curtains
(1983)
oil, 26.7 x 31.7 cm

Bright Blue Jug, White Mug
(1980/81)
oil, 29.9 x 38.8 cm

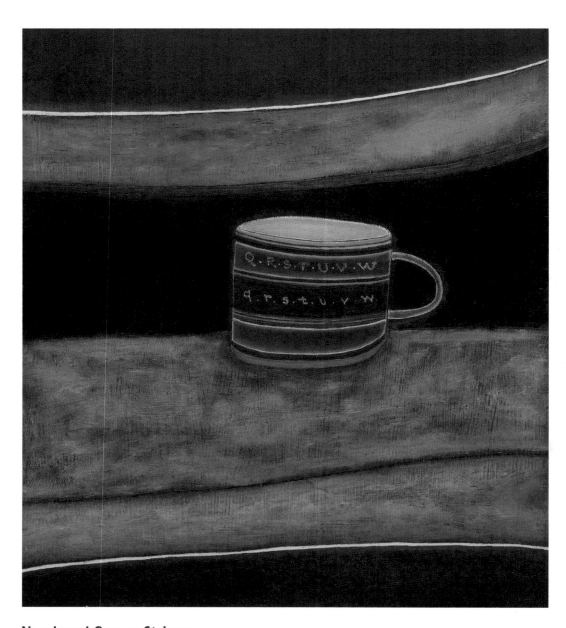

Numbered Cup on Stripes
(1979)
oil, 29.3 x 24.8 cm

Red Goblet, Blue Jug
(1983)
oil, 30.5 x 38.1 cm

Nottinghamshire
(1985)
acrylic, 22.9 x 29.3 cm

Derbyshire with Cows
(1986)
gouache, 20.9 x 29 cm

Barnaloft with Coffee Pot
(1986)
acrylic, 20.3 x 25.5 cm

Still life on Smoky Blue
(1984)
oil, 31.7 x 26.7 cm
PRIVATE COLLECTION

Still Life with Colander
(1981)
gouache, 10.4 x 21.6 cm

ANDREA FREARS

St Ives Fire Station
(1997)
acrylic, 20.3 x 38.1 cm

NORMAN POLLARD

Cornish Farms from Gurnards Head Hotel
(1986)
acrylic, 21.5 x 29.3 cm

A Yorkshire Landscape
(1988)
acrylic, 29.3 x 39.4 cm

View from 18 with Cups
(1987)
acrylic 17.8 x 25.5 cm

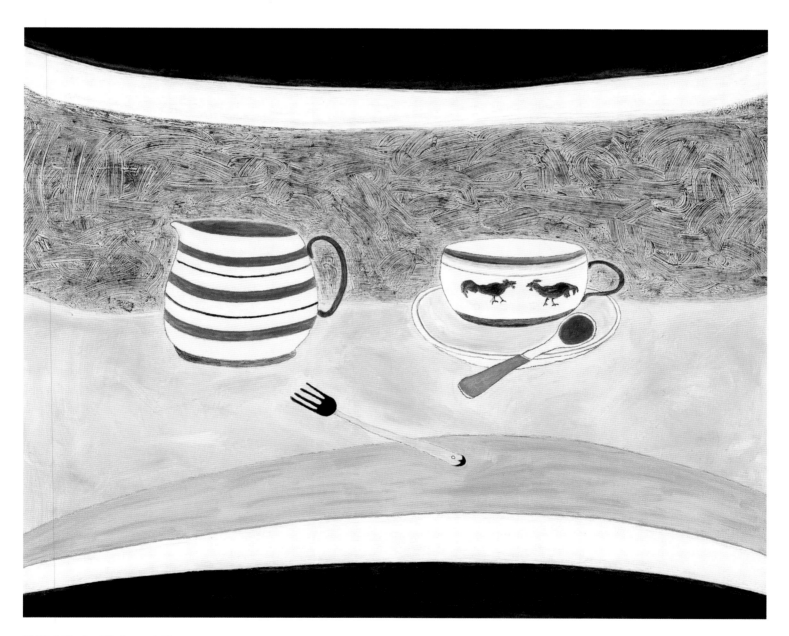

Still Life in Pink and Grey
(1992)
oil, 29 x 35 cm

NEW HALL, CAMBRIDGE UNIVERSITY

Derbyshire with Jugs
(1991)
acrylic, 25.5 x 35.6 cm

View from Pednolver Terrace
(1988)
acrylic, 40.6 x 30.5 cm

Striped Jug and Two Mugs
(1990)
oil, 25.4 x 36.5 cm

Composition on Brown and Black with Red Spoon
(1992)
lithograph (edition of 75), 25.5 x 20.3 cm (image size)
PRIVATE COLLECTION

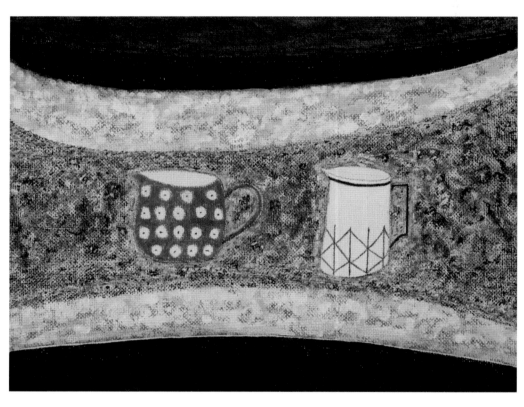

Still Life with Red
(1991–95)
acrylic, 15.2 x 20.3 cm

Museum Jug

(1992)

oil, 25.5 x 20.3 cm

PRIVATE COLLECTION

Landscape with Sheep, Dovedale
(1992)
oil, 30.5 x 41.6 cm

Cumbria in August
(1994)
acrylic, 30.5 x 40 cm

Theme on Striped Tea Cup and Flowered Mug
(1992)
oil, 29.9 x 37.4 cm

No.18 with Red Coffee Pot and Pebbles
(1989/90)
acrylic, 45.8 x 35.6 cm

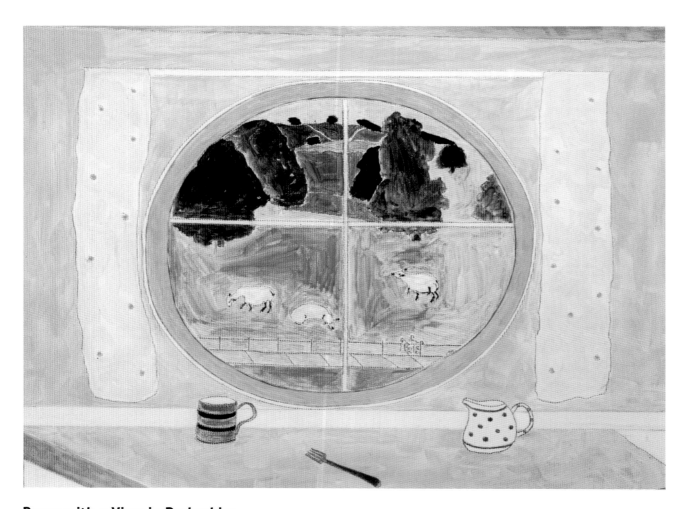

Room with a View in Derbyshire
(2000)
acrylic, 22.2 x 29.6 cm

Towards Coal Fell, Cumbria
(1994)
gouache, 22.9 x 28.7 cm

Barbara's Coffee Pot and Ben's Mug
(2005–08)
oil, 31.7 x 26.7 cm
PRIVATE COLLECTION

Coffee Pot and Jug
(1995–98)
oil, 29.9 x 37.4 cm

Towards Zennor
(1996)
acrylic, 45.8 x 61 cm

Bryher (Isles of Scilly)
(1999)
acrylic, 30.5 x 40 cm

Towards Thorpe Church (Derbyshire)
(1996)
gouache, 30.5 x 40.6 cm

View from D.H. Lawrence's House
(1996)
acrylic, 45.8 x 61 cm

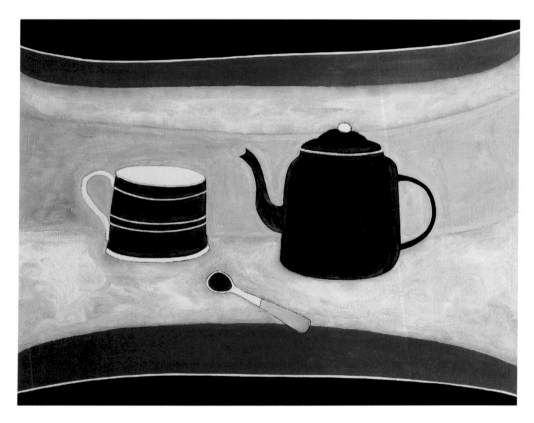

Three Objects on Smoky White
(1997)
oil, 29.9 x 37.4 cm

Five Objects with Spotty Jug
(1997)
oil, 45.8 x 61 cm

Autumn Still Life
(1996)
oil, 30.5 x 41.6 cm

Trencrom
(1997)
acrylic, 36.8 x 47 cm

View from Tate with Grey Table
(1997)
lithograph (edition of 75), 44 x 59 cm (image size)

Tate view from Corner Window 1
(1998)
acrylic, 58.8 x 61 cm

PRIVATE COLLECTION

Harbour with Still Life (St Ives)
(1999)
lithograph (edition of 100), 40.6 x 54 cm (image size)

FROM THE COLLECTION OF PAINTINGS IN HOSPITALS,
A CHARITY DEDICATED TO HEALTH AND WELL BEING

View from Park Terrace
(1997)
acrylic, 50.8 x 61 cm

Mullion
(2000)
acrylic, 22.9 x 29.6 cm

Another view from Joseph's
(2000/02)
gouache, 40.6 x 50.8 cm

View from Boveridge (Dorset)
(1998)
acrylic, 22.9 x 30.5 cm
PRIVATE COLLECTION

Restaurant View with Leach Jug
(1998)
gouache, 40.6 x 52 cm

View from Park Avenue
(2007)
acrylic, 45.8 x 61 cm

PRIVATE COLLECTION

View Towards Smeaton's Pier 2
(1999–2007)
acrylic, 40.6 x 50.8 cm

View down the Digey
(2003)
acrylic, 61 x 50.8 cm

View over Roof Tops
(1998–2000)
acrylic, 22.9 x 30.5 cm
PRIVATE COLLECTION

A Barnaloft Flat
(2001)
acrylic, 61 x 50.8 cm

Mousehole
(2000–05)
acrylic, 45.8 x 61 cm

Porthmeor View with Totem Pole
(2008)
gouache, 25.5 x 30.5 cm

Godrevy with Spotty Cup
(2003)
acrylic, 22.9 x 30.5 cm

Tall Spotty Jug with Red Spoon
(2004)
oil, 41.6 x 30.5 cm
PRIVATE COLLECTION

Green Tea Pot with Julia's Jug
(2005/06)
oil, 50.8 x 61 cm
PRIVATE COLLECTION

Blue, Yellow and Spots
(2000)
oil, 25.5 x 30.5 cm
PRIVATE COLLECTION

Spotty Mug on Black and Green
(2001)
acrylic, 25.5 x 20.3 cm

JON SNOW

Pink and Red
(2002—04)
oil, 43.5 x 61 cm

Blue Mug, Green Glass
(2003–05)
oil, 29.3 x 35.6 cm

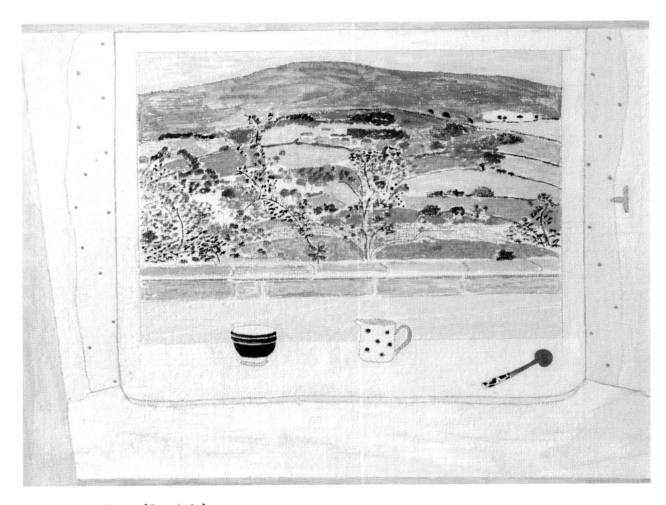

From Banks Head (Cumbria)
(2008)
gouache, 22.9 x 30.5 cm

Landscape near Biggin Hill (Derbyshire)
(2005/08)
acrylic, 30.5 x 40.6 cm

Towards the Island
(2006)
acrylic, 28 x 38.1 cm

Towards Rosewall with Still Life
(2008/09)
acrylic, 22.9 x 29.3 cm

Seascape with Blue
(2008)
oil pastel, 22.2 x 24.8 cm

Sailing Boat with Red Tea Pot and Orange and Black Mug
(2008)
oil pastel, 22.2 x 24.8 cm

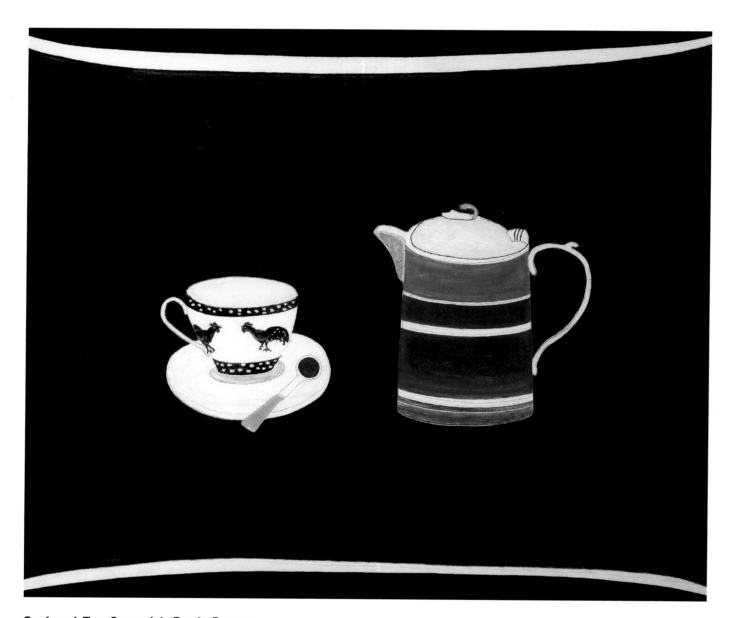

Cockerel Tea Cup with Ben's Pewter
(2008)
oil, 33 x 38.1 cm

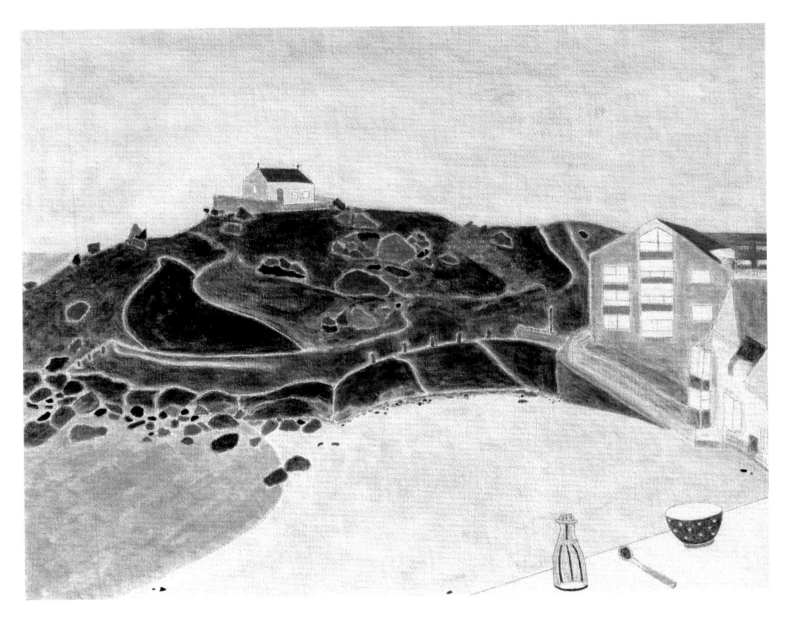

The Island with Decanter
(2005–07)
acrylic, 40 x 50.1 cm

Exhibitions

Solo exhibitions

1979 Field Gallery, Farnsfield,
Nottinghamshire
1980 Montpelier Studio, London
1982 Montpelier Studio
1985 Montpelier Studio
1988 Montpelier Studio
1990 Takanawa Gallery, Tokyo
1991 Montpelier Studio
1994 Montpelier Studio
1997 Montpelier Sandelson
2000 Montpelier Sandelson
2006 Caroline Wiseman Modern Art,
London

Mixed exhibitions

1976 to 2005
Wills Lane Gallery, St Ives
1981 Milton Keynes exhibition
1982 Beaux Arts, Bath. *Two Generations*
1981 Bath Contemporary Art Fair
1982 Bath Contemporary Art Fair
1983 Bath Contemporary Art Fair
1983 Crane Kalman: 'The Nicholsons'
1986 Wills Lane Gallery, St Ives:
'Four Painters: Patrick Hayman,
Andrew Lanyon, Rachel Nicholson
and John Wells'
1989 New Ashgate Gallery, Farnham:
'Anthony Bryant, Rachel Nicholson,
Tony O'Malley, Mary Rich'
1989 The City Gallery, Leicester
1993 Art Fair, Islington
1993 to 1998
New Academy Gallery:
'Curwen Chilford Prints'

1994 The City Gallery, Leicester
1994 The Coach House Gallery, Guernsey
1995 New Academy Gallery, London:
'Cornwall'
1995 Tate St Ives: 'Porthmeor Beach:
A Century of Images'
1996 Dartington Arts Gallery (with
Ffiona Lewis)
1996 The New Millennium Gallery, St Ives:
'Another View'
1997 New Academy Gallery, London
1997 20th Century British Art Fair
1998 20th Century British Art Fair
1998 Art Fair, Islington
1998 Tate St Ives: 'Partnerships and Practice'
(The role of Dartington Hall, Devon,
Bath Academy of Art, Corsham and
Leeds University in the lives of artists
mainly associated with St Ives)
1990 to the present
Thompson's, London, Aldeburgh and
Stow-on-the-Wold galleries
2000 Artmonsky, London
2000 to the present
Belgrave Gallery, St Ives
2001 Lynne Strover Gallery, Cambridgeshire
2003 Lemon Street Gallery, Truro
2003 British Art Fair, Commonwealth
Institute, London
2003 Lynne Strover Gallery, Cambridgeshire,
'Christmas Show'
2003 Caroline Wiseman Modern Art:
'Christmas Show' (principal artist)
2004 New Academy Gallery, London:
'Still-Life Exhibition'
2004 Art London
2004 British Art Fair, London

2004 Caroline Wiseman Modern Art:
'A Vital Simplicity: Four Generations
of the Nicholson Family'

2004 Caroline Wiseman Modern Art:
'Christmas Show'

2005 London Art Fair

2005 Fine Art Design and Antiques,
Olympia, London

2005 British Art Fair

2005 Caroline Wiseman Modern Art,
'St Ives to Newlyn' (the show also
toured to Eton College)

2005 Glyndebourne Gallery, Glyndebourne
Festival Opera Season

2005 Lynne Strover Gallery, Cambridge:
'Rose Rands and her Artist Friends'

2006 Lemon St Gallery, Truro

2006 Art Miami Art Fair, Miami

2007 Elizabeth Page Smith Gallery, Venice,
California: 'Family Garden Exhibition'
(to coincide with Venice Art Walk)

2007 Caroline Wiseman Modern Art:
'Christmas Show'

Prints

1992 *Composition on Brown and Black
with Red Spoon*, lithograph, Curwen
Chilford Prints Ltd

1997 *View from Tate with Grey Table*,
lithograph, Curwen Chilford
Prints Ltd

1999 *Harbour with Still Life (St Ives)*,
lithograph, Curwen Chilford
Prints Ltd, commissioned by
Paintings in Hospitals

Public collections

The Barns-Graham Charitable Trust
Chilwell Comprehensive School, Nottingham
Dartington Hall Trust
Paintings in Hospitals
New Hall, University of Cambridge

Biography

1934 Born Hampstead, London, 3 October, one of triplets, daughter of Barbara Hepworth and Ben Nicholson. Sent to Wellgarth Nursery Training College, London, with brother Simon and sister Sarah.

1937 Leave Wellgarth and go to 3 The Mall Studios, Hampstead with nurse and cook. Parents living in nearby 7 The Mall Studios.

1939 At the end of August, move to Carbis Bay near St Ives as guests of Adrian Stokes and his wife Margaret Mellis at Little Parc Owles. On 27 December, the Nicholsons move to a house called Dunluce, Carbis Bay.

1942 Early July, the Nicholson sign a seven-year lease on Chy-an-Kerris, Carbis Bay.

1944 to 1952: Aged ten, sent with Simon to Dartington Hall School. Sarah arrives a term later after being in hospital.

1953 to 1960: Attend management course for two years and later a secretarial course. Subsequently administration jobs until 1961.

1960 Marries Dr Michael Kidd, then teaching anatomy at University College, London. Later in a research post at Institute of Neurology, Maida Vale, London.

1961 Move to a 'Span' house in Blackheath, SE3.

1962 Jeremy born.

1964 Alison born.

1968 Julia born.

1969 Move to Bristol when husband takes teaching post at Bristol University Medical School.

1975 Move to Leicestershire when husband takes post as Senior Lecturer at Queen's Medical Centre, Nottingham University.

1975 Start painting.

1979 First solo exhibition at Field Gallery, Farnsfield, Nottinghamshire.

1980 First London solo exhibition at Montpelier Studio. Exhibit there for twenty years.

1982 Inherit father's Hampstead house and studio, 2B Pilgrims Lane, and commute there until 1985.

1985 Move to 2B Pilgrims Lane on husband's retirement. First proper studio.

1999 Start exhibiting at Thompson's, City Gallery, London, and later at their other London, Aldeburgh and Stow-on-the-Wold galleries.

2001 On account of husband's health, move to another house and studio in Hampstead.

2003 First exhibition with Caroline Wiseman Modern Art, London.

2006 Solo ehibition with Caroline Wiseman Modern Art.